THE SARASOTA SCHOOL OF ARCHITECTURE

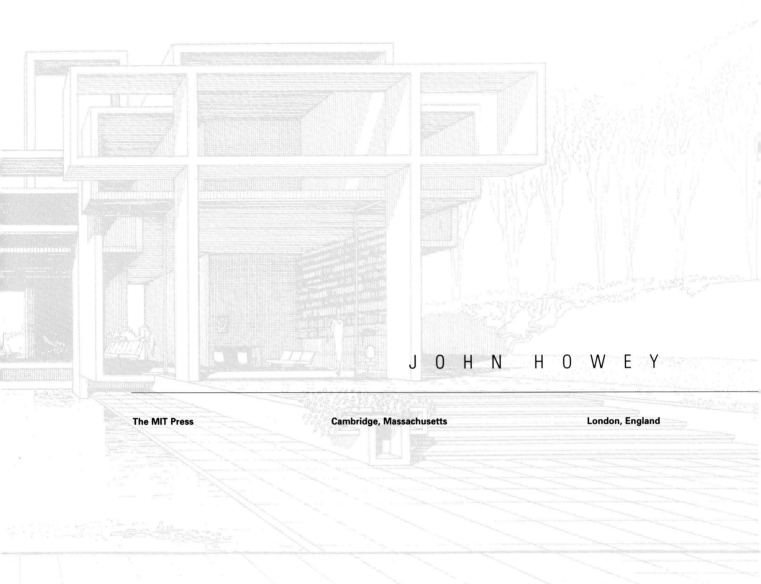

J O H N H O W E Y

The MIT Press   **Cambridge, Massachusetts**   **London, England**

Ralph S. Twitchell

Paul Rudolph

Ralph Zimmerman

William Zimmerman

Philip Hiss

Jack West

Gene Leedy

THE SARASOTA SCHOOL OF ARCHITECTURE

1 9 4 1 – 1 9 6 6

Mark Hampton

Phil Hall

Col. Roland Sellew

Tim Seibert

Victor Lundy

William Rupp

Joan and Ken Warriner

Tolyn Twitchell

Bert Brosmith

Frank Folsom Smith

Boyd Blackner

Louis Schneider

James Holiday

Joseph Farrell

Carl Abbott

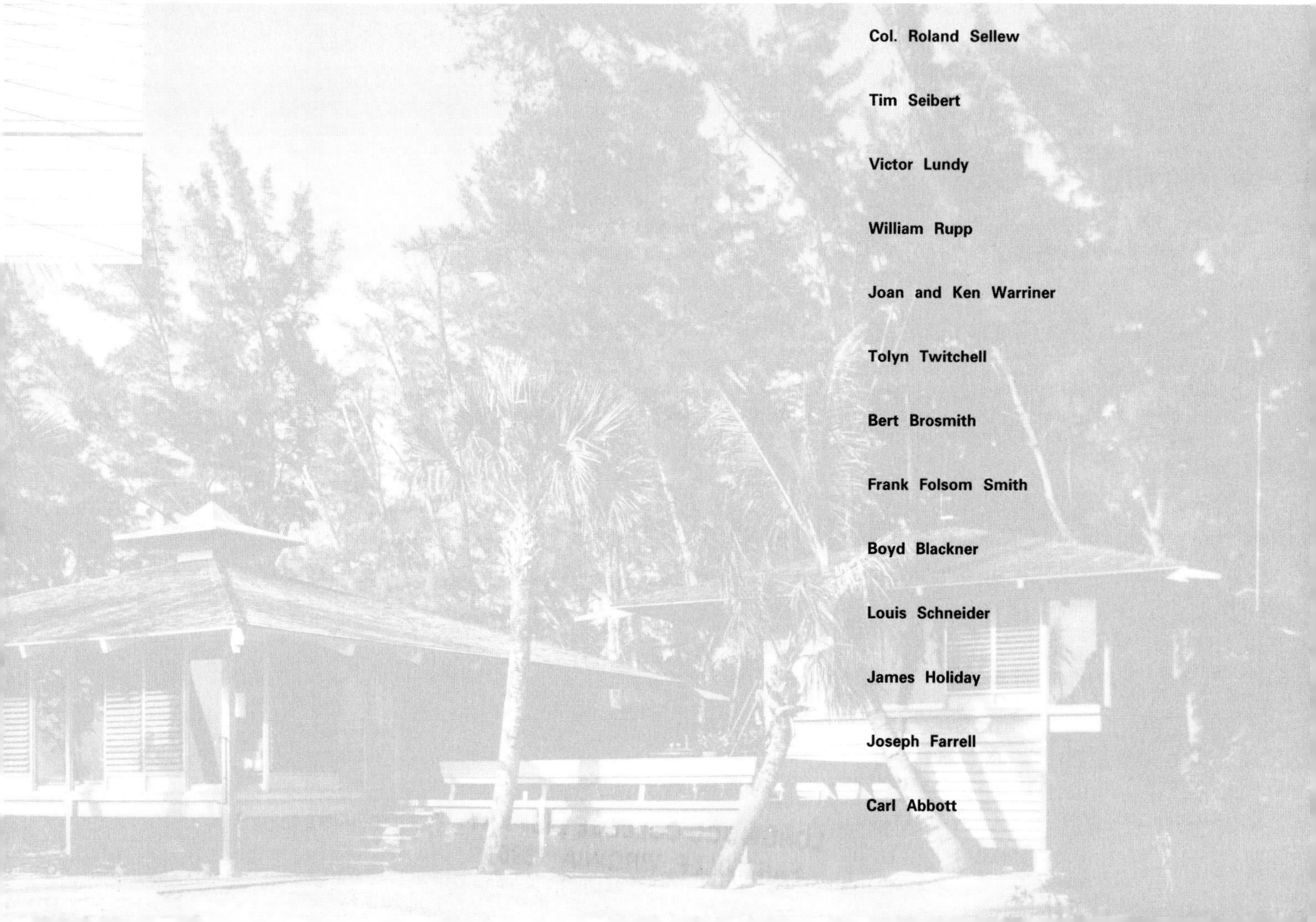

First MIT Press paperback edition, 1997

© 1995 Massachusetts Institute of Technology

This book was set in Univers by Graphic Composition, Inc., and was
printed and bound in the United States of America.

Library of Congress Cataloging-in-Publication Data

Howey, John.
    The Sarasota school of architecture : 1941–1966 / John Howey.
        p.   cm.
    Includes bibliographical references and index.
    ISBN 0-262-08240-3 (hc), 0-262-58156-6 (pb)
    1. Architecture, Domestic—Florida—Sarasota Region.   2. Architec-
ture, Modern—20th century—Florida—Sarasota Region.   3. Architecture—Florida—Sarasota Region.   I. Title.
NA7235.F62S265   1995
728'.37'09759610904—dc20   95-13652
                                                                  CIP

CONTENTS

FOREWORD: WHY SARASOTA?

Like all such conjunctions of time, place, and talent, this one has no ready formula, just a happy, alchemical precipitating longing for a perfect place in the sun. We're in Florida, after all, one of America's Ardens of charm, dream site since at least Ponce de León.

Utopia is always local: the indigenous raised to the flashpoint of vision. Sarasota's substrate of locality is compounded first of nature. A flatness extending over the white of the beach across the tepid waters of the aquamarine Gulf and ending in the spectacle of sunset. The unobstructed breeze when it blows. The tenuous length and small isolations of the battered keys. The tropical profligacy, the mangroves and the palms, the languor, the sweet rot.

Sarasota society supplied plenty of its own fantasies of possibility. The Palmers with their sun-stroked Trianon and monarchic acreage. The Ringlings—circus people, grandees of excess—abandoning the flimsy tensile big top of the northern summer for a mock solidity in the off-season south, gathering around them artists and *artistes,* giving this hot little spot a weird grandeur, a deluge of cash, and a kind of intellectual space that filled with students and writers, a torpid outpost of bohemia and quick-buck speculation. Philip Hiss, biker and free spirit, bourgeois Medici, citizen-patron, enthusiast, who insisted on architecture. And all those beachcombers and prospectors of paradise who simply liked the idea of living in this work.

The urbane Ralph Twitchell—acknowledged spark for all this—made Sarasota safe for modern architecture by embracing it. Building a house for McKinlay Kantor, he firmed up the alliance of architecture to art as it was happening, made the work not just a setting but an extension. He also yoked the hands-on, down and dirty discourse of the builder to the architecture of the town, created a way of making. Elder of the tribe, he must have conferred a remarkable tone and atmosphere on the activity of architecture, mixed the happy cocktail with a sure stir. And, of course, he hired Paul Rudolph fresh out of school.

Frank Lloyd Wright—that one-man fountain of youth—building nearby, both amplified the buzz and offered material models for construction, a useful tectonics. But it's another aspect of Wright's work that jibes especially with Sarasota's moment: his romance of the suburban deployments of the American middle class. That utopia was a new kind of paradise, distinctly American. The Sarasota architects built the Usonian shrines exalted by Wright, the modest houses, the public schools, the churches that formed the spine of postwar America's best idea of itself.

This was the surely ripest moment of high American modernism, and what was happening in Sarasota was mirrored around the country. Most kindredly and with likest latitude in Los Angeles in the work of Lautner and Soriano, Ellwood and Ain and all the other members of that great generation of architects that followed up the work of Schindler and Neutra and the ubiquitous Wright. Modernism adores a temperate climate and a shadow-crisping sun to allow its spaces to flow sure and clear. California and Florida shared for a time this free, hopeful, and leisured sense of possibility.

One of the great fascinations of paradise is the fall from it. Why did Sarasota end? The half-life of enthusiasm is part of it, the dulling of the optimism that followed the war. As the sixties progressed, America lost the confident lightness of functionalism as it careened into a fresh baroque of stupid prosperity. The stars—Rudolph and Victor Lundy—moved on to bigger ponds as the confines of Sarasota began to hem rather than stimulate. The locals became less hospitable, the spirit of the strip sapped the spirit of the place.

But the legacy remains, lovingly served and expanded by a handful of practitioners still there and recorded in its glorious variety and consistency in this long-needed book.

Michael Sorkin
New York/Vienna

INTRODUCTION

■ "We felt we had found 'The Answer'" is how a young architect captured the excitement and the commitment engendered by the new architecture of Sarasota in the late 1940s and the 1950s.[1] Indeed, this remembrance by William Rupp, who visited the offices of Ralph Twitchell and Paul Rudolph in 1950, could serve as the motto for this entire period of high modernism in America.

Few questioned that a bright and shining future lay ahead, that anything and everything seemed possible to those who were willing to project it. Who would not be dazzled by those strikingly linear drawings and the captivating photographs of this new architecture that seemed to have appeared as if by magic from one of the most unlikely of places, an architectural backwater known, if known at all, for its lavish revivalism of the 1920s? But then in the late 1930s a tentative new spirit had begun to appear that burst out after World War II. Thin frames, open walls, flat or curving roofs, floating furniture, and golden slippers; the building appeared to be suspended in space or floating above water—a modern hut in the tropics. Implicit is a sense of commitment; there on the west coast of Florida one could tangibly grasp the clarion call of the modern movement that had been argued about and struggled with for the previous half-century. In Sarasota modernism made a dramatic appearance. From abroad came interest and euphoria, as foreign architects and their magazines began to focus on what was happening in Florida. And on the more popular level the Museum of Modern Art and the homemaker press weighed in, portraying an architecture that seemed magical and new.[2]

As the modern architecture of the 1940s and 1950s begins to emerge from the miasma of reaction and misconception that all recent history—especially a radical and challenging period—undergoes, one can begin to gain a perspective on its goals, achievements, and failures. The story ranges from the Case Study group in Los Angeles, with members such as Charles Eames, Craig Elwood, and Raphael Soriano, to midwesterners such as George Fred and William Keck in Chicago, to Charles Goodman at Hollin Hills, Alexandria, Virginia, and Paul Rudolph in Sarasota. Their common emphasis on the open rectangular frame unites them and also points back to the impact of Mies van der Rohe's work. There were other competing interests: Frank Lloyd Wright, who acted as the spiritual head of a loose confederation that included both his former students such as Alden Dow and those with a sympathy toward the so-called "organic" like Bruce Goff in Oklahoma and William V. Kaiser in Wisconsin. In a broad sense all of these individuals belonged to modernism as it developed, and all subscribed to certain beliefs that included a new way of life, a developing technology, and also an element of fear.

Fear underlay a great deal of the modernist belief in making it new. Esther McCoy best summarized this when, describing the Case Study house program, she noted that John Entenza, the program's creator, worried "that architecture would regress when building was resumed at the end of the war."[3] Many of this generation believed that the great economic boom after World War I had snuffed out a vibrant American modernism, and feared that the forces of reaction—period-style historicism—would return and reign again after World War II. The great evil lay with the use of the styles, and hence committed modernists demonized the use of historical quotation in design. Although for some this came to mean the employment of a singular architectural model—the flat-roofed box—not all agreed. Paul Rudolph criticized this "timid, monotonous thing" and the similar-looking Gropius boxes that sprang up around the world. In a 1957 article he advised architects to look at the historical building types of their region, for instance in the South the raised cottage, the open side or dog trot, the use of grilles, and other features that he had abstracted for his houses.[4]

Modernism meant a commitment to a new way of life, however hazy and ill-defined, not just modern architecture but literature, art, furniture, tableware, and politics. The buildings with their "openness," the so-called "free plan," the combination of spaces and walls of glass, all indicated that a different style of life was expected of the inhabitants. One of the features that stands out is the liberal progressivism not just of the architects but of many of the clients, as in Sarasota with the Healys and Phil Hiss. A corollary of modernism believed in the rational being and that through shared agreement the government at all levels could engender a more fair and equitable life for all.

Most of the architects and clients were positivists; they believed in the future and hoped to anticipate tomorrow through a commitment to advanced technology. Throughout the 1930s and then especially during World War II, when many of the architects worked in industry and construction, the anticipation grew: how could the new technology be applied? What came to be viewed as modern technology encompassed the fact applied as symbol. Paul Rudolph amply indicates this view in his recounting of the catenary-curved roof form of the Healy guest house: "It had to do purely with the idea of using the least material possible and making it as light as possible and as efficient as possible, the whole notion of it being structurally clear. I was profoundly affected by ships. . . . I remember thinking that a destroyer was one of the most beautiful things in the world. I still think that. The whole notion of tension structures which you find in ships . . . because they're light in weight."[5] At the same time this was perhaps overdoing it, as Rudolph admitted: "It should have been used on a building with a 300-ft. span, but I just couldn't wait."[6] In retrospect it is obvious that the committed modernists were correct in some of their assumptions and fears and wrong in others. The emphasis upon tectonics over economics helps define this period of modernism and also indicates its shortsightedness.

The annual architectural honor awards that began in 1948 under the sponsorship of *Progressive Architecture* and then were picked up by the AIA in 1949, along with the ensuing *PA* design awards begun in 1955, illustrate the dominance of modernism; little that can be called historicist appears for the next several decades. Among many awards, Twitchell and Rudolph received an AIA award of merit in 1950 for the Healy guest house; Rudolph won an AIA honor award in 1962 for the Sarasota High School and received *PA*'s first design award in 1955 for the Cohen residence.[7] In architecture schools the old Beaux-Arts-based system largely disappeared, and although remnants remained, such as an emphasis on the plan or on architecture as a fine art, the new dress was unabashedly modern.

Unfortunately, this modernist focus on tectonics, form, and fine art served increasingly to marginalize the architectural profession as a provider of housing for the middle class. The vast pent-up demand for housing unleashed at the end of World War II coupled with low interest rates brought to the housing scene a new force, the "merchant builder," or developer.[8] Most famously exemplified by William Levitt and his various Levittowns, a transformation occurred across the United States as suburban housing tracts sprouted from former farm land. Most merchant builders viewed architects with suspicion if not hostility; as one developer explained: "Plans were drawn by a draftsman or a building designer who specialized in such work."[9]

A few architects recognized the challenge and tried to respond to the new order, such as Charles Goodman who associated with National Homes Corporation to design a series of prefabricated models. Out in the San Francisco Bay area, S. Robert Anshen and Stephen Allen designed a notable series of modern tract houses for Joseph Eichler.[10] Other architects attempted to combat the predominance of developer housing, such as Paul Rudolph with his various modular housing projects that employed what he called the "Twentieth Century Brick": prefabricated trailers. This idea was never fully realized. It is unfortunately too true that many of the houses of the Sarasota school were second homes, in a sense not intended for year-round living, and the clientele for them was limited. The impact of the developer *sans* architect appears all too frequently in Sarasota and its surroundings. In its native haunt the Sarasota school now appears as an archaeological artifact overwhelmed by suburban boxes.

Whether the Sarasota school made a lasting impact is open to question. There is an American tradition that stretches well back into the nineteenth century in which the planning and architecture of summer communities becomes the ideal for the American middle-class suburb. Some features of the Sarasota school houses (and also common to other modernists) did enter mainstream American housing: the glass wall became sliding doors opening on the rear yard, the open plan became that vast space of the family-kitchen room, the merging of indoors and outdoors appeared as the deck. All of these features and more derived from the modernist revolution became staples of the developer's house, even as the outer garb could be anything under the sun.

The causes for, and the debate over, the relative failure of post–World War II American modernism have been a feature of architectural writing for the past twenty years.[11] Nothing succeeds like a harsh and bitter attack; the failures of modern architecture—like the disappointments of big government—are very easy to identify for the opportunistic quick hit. The alternative, the naive meliorism of many modernist supporters, seems equally unsatisfactory. What has been missing and what this book helps to restore is the question of the relative success of the actual buildings.

The Sarasota school encompassed more than just houses, and other notable talents besides Rudolph and Twitchell. How much it can really be called a school is questionable, since the various designs of Victor Lundy exude an expressionist stance more akin to the projects of Bruce Goff, or of Erich Mendelsohn just after World War I. Although a common vision is not always so apparent, Sarasota provided the right climate for an architectural flowering. The variety of expression shown in Sarasota personifies the changing and exploratory nature of American modernism in these years.

Rudolph actually began as a Wrightian during his initial architectural training at Alabama Polytechnic Institute, but then the Harvard years under Gropius shoved him into a tight rectangular frame. By the mid-1950s, however, Rudolph's earlier proclivities began to resurface, possibly spurred both by the example of Lundy and the postwar work of Le Corbusier. Corbusier's seemingly sudden transformation from the rigid mechanophile modernism typified in his work of the 1920s to the free sculptural forms of his postwar work shocked many architects.[12] Rudolph left the International Style box far behind with the Milam and Wallace residences, the Sarasota High School, and ultimately Yale's Art and Architecture Building.

Today, with the advantage of nearly four decades of perspective, Rudolph's position appears prescient. Although his criticism came from a modernist perspective, he sensed the vapid banality emanating from orthodox modernism as it developed.[13] The most restless of his generation, Rudolph attempted to break the orthodox stranglehold with his various experiments in roof forms, fenestration, and selective contextual abstraction. His Jewett Arts Center at Wellesley College from the same period illustrates his attempt to tie into the neo-Gothic campus and indicates the cracks already appearing in the modernist cry to "make it new." To label the Jewett as postmodern is inaccurate, but it is a nascent example. Away from Sarasota, Rudolph's quest culminated with the Yale Art and Architecture Building. Castigated and defiled over the years, the Yale building is certainly one of the landmarks of this bygone era.

How much has been lost of these years is graphically apparent in this book; many of the houses in Sarasota are either destroyed or altered beyond recognition. Nostalgia, however, is not what the book is about. The great value of this account is that John Howey approaches the subject as an architect, understanding the technical and programmatic issues that guided the designers. He clearly shows that, while Sarasota began to appear on the architectural radar in 1945, a tradition of innovative architecture had existed there from its beginning. Having designed numerous buildings in the same area, Howey speaks from a point of architectural awareness. He convincingly outlines the genesis of the Sarasota school that made the world sit up and take notice.

Richard Guy Wilson
University of Virginia

ACKNOWLEDGEMENTS

■ Many participated in the effort to make this book a reality. From the initial encouragement Gene Leedy gave me to undertake this adventure to the final interviews with the people involved, I learned much about the Sarasota school of architecture. Patty Jo Rice, Paula Twitchell, Jack Twitchell, Sylva Hutchinson, Lu Andrews, Shirley Hiss, David Lindsey, Wilson Stiles, Ben Baldwin, Ann Shank, Harriet Burket Taussig, Robert Ivy, Richard Guy Wilson, Robert McCarter, Peter Smithson, Michael Sorkin, Jeff LaHurd, Phil Hammill, Chris Risher, Tom Marvel, Bill Morgan, Bob Broward, Jim Cary, Mildred Schmertz, Gail and Paul Whiting, William Raley, Donald Mitchell, Carl Strang, Max Strang, David Crane, John and Safie Ellerman, and my wife, Maria, supplied information, sometimes photographs, and enthusiasm during this journey.

My appreciation goes to Mary Beth Harris, Jennifer Parmer, Susan McCarty, and Erin McDuffie, who labored with my drafts to put the manuscript into its final form.

A special thank-you goes to the current owners of Sarasota school buildings for their willingness to allow visits, and, in some cases, measurements and photographs at their sites.

Others particularly helpful were the Sarasota Department of Historical Resources, the Sarasota City Clerk's office, the Gulf Coast Chapter of the American Institute of Architects, and, finally, the architects who are the subjects of the book, who sometimes lent their *only* photograph or drawing (with threat of death if not returned!) to make its publication possible. With so many generous people, I am sure I have missed noting someone who was vital to the book's progress. So thank you, too.

The writing and publication of this book have been aided by a generous grant from the Graham Foundation for Advanced Studies in the Fine Arts.

J.H.

THE SARASOTA SCHOOL OF ARCHITECTURE

CHAPTER ONE

PHILOSOPHIES AND RESULTS

Paradise, the pinnacle of place, is often found in the imagination. Much rarer is an actual location close to perfection, a spot capable of arousing the higher intellect and emotion in a large group of people living there. Sarasota, Florida, is such a place. The Sarasota school sprang out of its special circumstances of location, personalities, and talent to reach its zenith of world architectural prominence in the 1950s. For postwar Sarasota, the task was to create the better place, to delineate and define itself in this unique tropical environment that existed nowhere else in the United States.

Ralph Twitchell and Paul Rudolph together began an indigenous Florida West Coast architecture based on shared beliefs. It started with Twitchell's respect for the land and the climate, appreciation for what was good from the past, eye for local materials, and use of new construction techniques. In 1941 Paul Rudolph arrived with his enormous design talent, an awareness of changing cultural values, and his aggressive desire to probe the immediate architectural future. Twitchell had already acquired his educational, social, and cultural training by then; Rudolph was about to complete his. Earnest and honest, their initial philosophy was formulated by Rudolph in 1947:

1. Clarity of construction

2. Maximum economy of means

3. Simple overall volumes penetrating vertically and horizontally

4. Clear geometry floating above the Florida landscape

5. Honesty in details and in structural connections[1]

Through their early designs, starting with the Finney residence project in 1947, Twitchell and Rudolph began to verbally articulate their visual expressions with a taut modernist language. The two were able to indicate clearly their new architectural direction (figure 1.1).

New technology made their advanced ideas feasible. In the Finney project, newly available large fixed glass panels exposed the house's beamed roof with wide cantilever overhangs to unobstructed views on all sides. Non-loadbearing privacy walls with high horizontal clear glass bands between

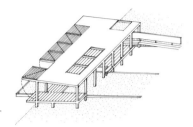

1.1 | **Finney residence,** Siesta Key, 1947

1.2 | **Healy "Cocoon House,"** Siesta Key, 1948–1950

1.3 | **Golden Gate Bridge,** San Francisco, 1936

wall and roof further separated the body of the house from its roof and created the feeling of horizontal planes floating in space. To heighten the transparency, glass casement windows were framed into the fixed glass walls for ventilation. (Neither air conditioning nor large sliding glass doors were yet commercially available in 1947.)[2]

The next leap into the future was the 1948–1950 Healy guest house (figure 1.2). The "Cocoon House," as it was called, embodied technology the military used in mothballing ships and airplanes. In this structure the floating roof is hung from two edge beams as a sagging catenary, made of thin steel straps supporting curved fiberboard and insulation panels, sealed with a sprayed-on outer plastic roof. The idea appears to have evolved from 1930s suspension bridges (figure 1.3). Also unique was the introduction of operating wood or glass jalousie window units set floor to ceiling, privacy walls that with the turn of a crank were totally opened to breezes, light, and views. The house sits above a plane of sand and over a seawall, surrounded not by vegetation but by sky and water, as Twitchell and Rudolph stressed in a 1951 description of its siting: "In a sense this is an antisocial building, for it ignores the neighboring assortment of non-committal

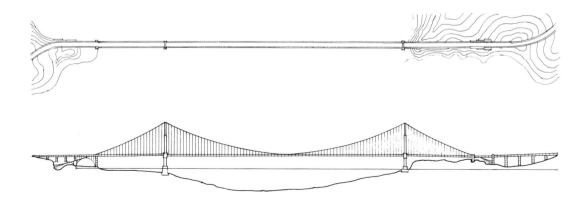

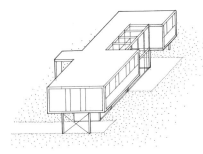

houses. It can even be said that it dominates the bayou, because of its placement, form, color and materials. The surrounding structures are already covered with a profusion of lush growth; in this cottage, however, we wanted to demonstrate that harmony between the work of nature and the work of man can be brought about by clearly differentiating between the two."[3] So unusual was this beach house for its time that it immediately gained attention world wide.[4]

A series of simple wood, glass, and concrete-block structures exemplified Twitchell and Rudolph's postwar architectural thought. Several features made them regional: native materials such as local cypress were used; floors were often raised to avoid the Florida dampness; a typically southern dogtrot was used to obtain maximum interior ventilation; the chimney was placed tangential to and separate from the main structure; windows, grilles, and shutters were used to filter the intense light and help control the sun; and other basic building components were separated to lessen heat transfer and to break down the sun's rays before they penetrated glass or struck exterior walls. Modular construction of these components facilitated their use.

Thus vernacular Floridian architectural ideas tied to southern regional traditions contributed to Twitchell and Rudolph's indigenous solutions. Patios, courts, screened porches, verandas, open plans, free flowing of inner and outer spaces, and lightness of structure were adapted to their Sarasota work.

Gradually a series of thematic ideas and practices developed from their basic tenets and from other Sarasota architects began to contribute to the process of defining a "Sarasota group":

1. The main mass of the house was raised to the second level for better views and breezes and sun protection below. The upper level was wood-framed. The lower parts were often masonry (figure 1.4).

2. On his own, Rudolph developed flexed quarter-inch plywood roof vaults to shelter living spaces (figure 1.5).

3. Two- or three-story-high shells or upper umbrella roofs evolved to protect or enclose the smaller living units underneath (figure 1.6).

4. Rudolph used hinged shutters or "flaps" so large in scale that they became major building units and could change the perception of the whole structure when pivoted up or down (figure 1.7).

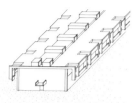
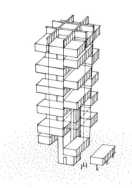
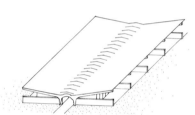

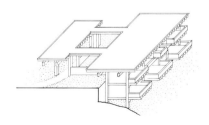

5. The group successfully adapted these structural and regional components to larger-scale projects (figure 1.8).

6. Technological concepts were transformed into useful urban architectural forms (figure 1.9).

7. Floating sculptural forms were used for contrast with the flat Florida landscape (figure 1.10).

8. Lightweight laminated wood, concrete, steel, and air structural systems were used by Victor Lundy in his architecture (figure 1.11).

9. Precast, prestressed concrete structural systems were developed scaled to Florida residences by Gene Leedy (figure 1.12).

10. Florida interior design and detailing was refined.

The resultant work showed that the architects shared an unspoken consensus, reinforced by a community-wide aesthetic enthusiasm and sense of place in Sarasota among photographers, musicians, actors, writers, and artists.[5]

What makes the Sarasota group's work constitute a school of architecture like the "Prairie school" or the "Philadelphia school"? It is first the individuals involved: Ralph Twitchell, the acknowledged father of the school, and Paul Rudolph, its spiritual leader. Their bold architectural work and theories were advanced and added to by the prominent group members Mark Hampton, Gene Leedy, and Jack West, and the separate genius of Victor Lundy. The group was centered in a particular city, Sarasota, and region, the Florida West Coast, and it lasted for 25 years. It was an active, unified group that regarded architecture as an art form and that took advantage of structural evolution and new technology. Its work shared the principles of the earlier Chicago and Prairie schools. Finally, it had the vitality to spread to a larger group of students and architects in Florida during the decade of the 1950s. Its spirit and energy created national and international attention that continues to this day.[6]

Sarasota at midcentury showed that a unique new architectural heritage could develop in a special place and offer fresh social, economic, political, and historical ideas. The details of this movement and these contributions are examined in the following chapters.

CHAPTER TWO

EARLY SARASOTA

Origins

Bordered by more shorelines, bays, and beaches than any other state in the United States, Florida is a lush, humid, tropical peninsula inhabited by panthers, bears, armadillos, alligators, snakes, and mosquitos (figure 2.1). Racked by intense summer heat and humidity and pounded by annual seasons of tropical storms and hurricanes, this sometimes hostile place seemed unlikely to invite the unparalleled population growth it has seen this century. Sarasota, located midway down the peninsula on the Gulf of Mexico, also appeared an unlikely place for the architectural movement it spawned (figure 2.2). What, then, created the atmosphere for Sarasota's growth and creative architectural energy?

2.1   **NASA photo of Florida peninsula,** 1966

2.2   **View of a Sarasota bayou,** 1950

2.3 | **Fort San Marcos,** c. 1672, St. Augustine, Florida

2.4 | **Gamble Mansion,** 1844, Ellenton, Florida

2.5 | **View from Sarasota pier to DeSoto Hotel and Five Points,** 1887

Native Americans left the first mark on the landscape, but their only permanent remains were seashell middens near its shoreline. Spanish explorers led by Hernando de Soto and his followers came by ship, landing in the Sarasota-Bradenton area in 1539. Over the next two centuries, Spanish colonists built forts, missions, and small homes using indigenous coquina rock and cedar. Little from this era exists today. In St. Augustine, Florida, the oldest colonial city in the United States, founded by the Spanish in 1565, Fort San Marcos remains from that time (figure 2.3). While this first architecture was largely utilitarian, the Spanish colonial heritage was remembered years later in what was called Mediterranean Revival architecture.

Florida fell to English rule in 1767, only to be ceded back to Spain in 1783. The colony was finally sold to the United States in 1819 after English and

Spanish authority had been reduced by colonial revolution. The Territory of Florida was established in 1822, and it became a state in 1845.

Access to Sarasota Bay was mainly by ship, although some rough trails were cleared in the interior. In 1824, when Fort Brooke was built near Tampa as a U.S. military outpost, Sarasota existed as a fishing village. As more visitors and settlers arrived, several plantations were established in the area, producing sugarcane, cotton, cattle, and hogs. Citrus groves and guavas were planted with seeds brought from Cuba.

Still standing is the Gamble mansion and its once self-sufficient plantation in nearby Ellenton, Florida (figure 2.4).[1] Designed in 1844, the main house is a typical Southern tabby masonry and stucco two-story Greek Revival

structure, one room wide, with porches on three sides. Cooking and other service activities were carried out in an adjacent building to the rear.

In the 1860s, the Civil War brought a hiatus in growth. In 1881, Hamilton Disston purchased 4 million acres for $1 million from the nearly bankrupt state of Florida, including much land in and around Sarasota. Three years later a Scottish syndicate headed by Sir John Gillespie bought 60,000 acres from Disston, comprising the site of Sarasota to the bay. Sixty Scottish families were sent there to establish a colony that brought the construction of a post office, a three-hole golf course, and the first Sarasota hotel, the DeSoto (figure 2.5).[2] Transportation was still almost entirely by water, with connections to steamers operating in and out of Tampa.

2.6   **Plant Hotel,** Tampa, Florida,1892

2.7   **Ponce de Leon Hotel,** built to serve new railroad built by Flagler, St. Augustine, Florida, 1890

In the 1880s, Florida's warm climate, clear water, beaches, ports, and tropical growth began to attract a new type of speculator: the railroad developer. Sensing the potential of expansion into Florida, rail entrepreneur Henry Plant had built a line from Jacksonville to Tampa by 1886. Plant saw the prospects of tourism and connecting with international commerce at his Gulf port (figure 2.6). On the east coast, Henry Flagler was also extending his railroad southward to Miami and Key West (figure 2.7). Land promotion and acquisition became a wild speculative adventure in Florida. Fantasyland in Utopia had begun.

In 1899, Sarasota was a five-block-long community of only 20 houses, without sidewalks but with a nine-hole golf course, and was known in the North as a fishing and golf resort. By 1909, there was electricity, a paved Main Street, and a narrow hard-surfaced road from Sarasota to Bradenton. This was a time of population growth and construction. In 1911, Mrs. Potter Palmer (figure 2.8), of Chicago banking and society, purchased 26,000 acres near Sarasota. Her program of farming, road building, and development was ambitious and successful. Through her efforts, a Sarasota winter social season began. She was the first to generate local culture in this sleepy resort town.

Holabird and Roche, well-known Chicago architects, designed a Sarasota mansion for Mrs. Palmer in 1912. With three stories, 30 rooms, and provisions for an elevator, this proposed reinforced concrete structure would if built have rivaled later Sarasota projects of the 1920s (figure 2.9).[3] Mrs. Palmer's death in 1918 put an end to this project, though her family continued many of the other Palmer Sarasota activities.

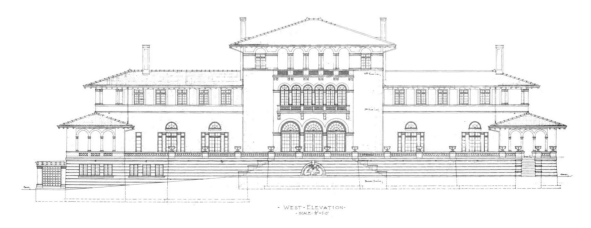

· WEST · ELEVATION ·
· SCALE · ⅛" = 1'-0" ·

2.8 **Mrs. Potter Palmer**

2.9 **Proposed Palmer mansion,** 1912 (unbuilt)

Also in 1912, John Ringling visited Sarasota (figure 2.10). The next year his brother, Charles Ringling, arrived with him and they bought adjoining "cottages" with waterfront property. This was the beginning of Sarasota's 50-year relationship with the Ringlings and the circus. On January 1, 1914, Sarasota was incorporated as a city and its first mayor was elected. In 1916, an opera hall opened to a full house.

World War I caused many wealthy families to vacation in Florida rather than Europe. By the end of the war, resort construction had changed from mostly wood frame to the more substantial masonry and stucco Spanish Mediterranean style promoted by Palm Beach society architect Addison Mizner (figure 2.11). It became popular to build one's own Florida mansion for the winter season. A new wave of speculation in Florida and Sarasota began.

2.10 | **John Ringling**

2.11 | **Gulfstream Golf Club,** Gulfstream, Florida, 1923; Addison Mizner, architect

Boom Time

In 1920 the big Florida land boom was just beginning to be noticeable in Sarasota. Each winter the number of tourists increased there. A slow but steady rise in real estate property values occurred. Utopia again beckoned and promoters of Florida fantasy responded.

Two visionaries encouraged by the Sarasota situation were John and Charles Ringling, whose empire began with show business, railroads, and banking. With winter residences in Sarasota, they now added beachfront real estate, hotels and the arts to their acquisitions and activities. The brothers, ideally suited for the roaring twenties, managed to purchase nearly all of the islands fronting Sarasota on the bay, facing the Gulf of Mexico, thus controlling most of the prime Gulf-front property. Undaunted by a 1921 hurricane, the brothers began dredging operations to turn their mangrove flats into solid land. The process consisted of subdividing the land into rows of lots, then cutting access canals between rows, and using the fill obtained from these canals to raise the elevation of the lots. Crude concrete seawalls, many of which later proved unsatisfactory, were originally constructed to hold the new land created for building. A causeway and bridge were built to the islands.

The appearances of Bird, St. Armands, and Lido keys, Cedar Point, and the southern end of Longboat Key were drastically changed. St. Armands Circle was designed to accommodate upscale shops and restaurants on St. Armands Key. Landscaping, Italian statuary, palm-lined boulevards, canals, sewers, and water mains were installed on these keys.

During Sarasota's 1922–1923 winter season, real estate activity increased dramatically. Subdivisions proliferated, lot prices escalated, and paper profits pyramided. Irresponsible, rampant speculation disregarded the local limitations of land, water, and ecology. In architecture, past European styles and pieces of buildings were borrowed at a hectic rate. Moorish, Spanish Colonial, Mission, and Italianate—with Hellenic thrown in for good measure—constituted the Mediterranean Revival style boom in Florida. This eclecticism practiced in California and Palm Beach now became the popular statewide Florida style.[4] There was not enough time or desire to invent a Florida architecture.

A friendly rivalry existed between the Ringling brothers. Each owned his own bank, real estate development company, and hotel. Their rivalry peaked in 1925 with the designs of their respective mansions, which replaced earlier cottages. Charles built a magnificent marble Georgian palace; nearby, John outdid him with an extravagant Venetian palazzo called Ca'd'Zan ("House of John" in the Venetian dialect of Italian) (figure 2.12).

2.12   **Ca'd'Zan,** Sarasota, 1926; Dwight James Baum, architect

2.13   **Peter Paul Rubens,** *The Three Graces,* 1639

The four-story structure (counting the viewing tower) faces Sarasota Bay with an enormous 8,000-square-foot marble terrace that also acts as a boat dock on the water. During its construction, John and Mabel Ringling chartered an entire freighter in Europe, filled it with artwork by Rubens, Titian, and Rembrandt purchased there, as well as statuary, doorways, arches, tiles, columns, and stonework, and shipped it all to the United States to be incorporated in their mansion and other Sarasota development projects (figure 2.13).

Basically, Ca'd'Zan is of reinforced concrete with its exterior walls stuccoed and ornamented with decorative glazed and colored terracotta tiles. The roofs are of Italian clay tiles, the windows of Venetian colored glass. Inside, a large skylight illuminates the two-story ceiling of the great hall. Surrounding the hall are many balconies and some 30 rooms comprising the mansion. More balconies, arches, and frescoed ceilings are found in the lesser spaces. The pecky cypress in the coffered ceilings was the only Florida material used in the mansion.[5]

Dwight James Baum of New York was John Ringling's architect for Ca'd'-Zan, and architect Ralph Twitchell (figure 2.14) was hired to represent Baum in Sarasota during its final construction phase. Pressed to complete Ca'd'Zan by the winter of 1926, Twitchell impressed the Ringlings with his resourcefulness in commandeering railroad cars from California to carry the necessary onyx columns to finish the mansion on time.[6] This close relationship between Twitchell and the Ringling family continued into the 1930s.

1925 proved to be the height of Sarasota's boom. The city attorney drafted a Greater Sarasota Charter, enacted November 22, 1925. This statute increased the city's size from its original two square miles to 69 square miles, with the new Classical county courthouse by Baum located downtown. The Sarasota Realty Board hastily published an atlas in an effort to locate the numerous new subdivisions.

By 1926 Florida began to have financial problems. Signs of economic stress appeared. First, the state rail system failed when there were insufficient tracks and rail workers to move goods. With the lack of materials, construction stopped and builders began going bankrupt. Second, the Florida real estate market acquired a bad reputation because of misrepresentations

2.14 **Ralph Twitchell**, 1926

made by overzealous salespeople and outright con men. New investors hesitated and financial brokers began to withdraw support. Third, natural disasters affected the Florida economy. A destructive hurricane hit Miami on September 26, 1926; damage totaled $76 million. In 1927, the Mediterranean fruit fly destroyed much of the state's citrus crop, and in 1928 a second hurricane hit south Florida, killing nearly 2,000 people at Lake Okeechobee. Because of these events, Florida entered the depression before the rest of the United States. Architects like Baum and Twitchell, with no prospects of local work, left the state.

The boom had lasted seven short years in Sarasota. Many projects were left unfinished. Two major banks failed by 1929. And yet the city was left with three large new hotels, a new downtown with two high-rise blocks, scores of apartment buildings, hundreds of new homes, a new hospital, an excellent school system, parks, playgrounds, a municipal golf course, and 77 miles of paved streets. A paved highway now connected Sarasota directly with the eastern coast and the Tamiami Trail now linked Tampa, Sarasota, and Miami. 1929 was a time for retrenching and recovery.

Depression

Limbo best describes the state of Florida in 1930. There was no new construction in Sarasota. Ringling Causeway was closed because of rotting bridge planks, for there was no money to replace them. St. Armands Key, subdivided into building lots during the previous decade, became a wasteland of statues and street curbs overgrown with high grass.

Yet in Sarasota, winter activity occurred where Ringling Causeway met downtown and the bay. The circus arrived for the winter in 1929–1930, and John Ringling, as yet unaffected by the economy, continued construction of the Florentine-style art museum and school he and his late wife, Mabel, had begun in 1928 (figure 2.15). A municipal airport with grass runways was built next to the circus grounds. The Chicago Palmers acquired the defunct First Bank and Trust Company and renamed it Palmer Bank.

The atmosphere of cultural sophistication and acquisition now surrounding the Ringlings' projects attracted artists, writers, designers, and musicians to the area. The opening of the junior college for teaching the arts in 1931 gave a further boost to these interests. After the dedication, John Ringling turned over the museum, the junior college (later called Ringling School of Art), and his art to the Southern Methodist Church of Lakeland, Florida. Church officials were mortified, however, when they later discovered on visiting the school that the student art classes included drawing live nudes. Showing a remarkable lack of foresight, they gave everything back to Ringling.[7] The art, the museum, and the mansion, now owned by the state of Florida, are valued at over $100 million.

2.15 | **Ringling Museum,** Sarasota, 1930; John Hyde Phillips, architect

Nationally, critics such as Henry-Russell Hitchcock were now promoting the new Modern architectural movement. Hitchcock teamed with Alfred Barr and Philip Johnson to stage the influential New York Museum of Modern Art exhibit on International Style Architecture in 1932, which encouraged Americans to look at and incorporate these new forms in architecture.

1932 saw the arrival of federal relief funds. Sarasota's first "made work" project was the repair of Ringling Causeway. In 1933, the Civilian Works Administration started local projects. Most influential was the Works Project Administration (WPA), which started building roads and parks in 1935 and constructing public buildings soon after.[8]

The Ringling enterprises began to suffer setbacks as the depression persisted. The decline in the circus business, the failure of their two Sarasota banks in 1932 and 1933, and Mabel and Charles Ringling's deaths helped to alienate John Ringling from the other family stockholders. While in New York in 1936 trying to raise money to regain control of the circus and to save his Sarasota home from the Internal Revenue Service, Ringling died at the age of 70. With his death an era had ended, but the Ringlings' legacy to the arts and the circus continues to benefit the community.

Recovery

Two events in the late 1930s had a fundamental impact on the course of architecture in Sarasota. The first was the 1936 rearrival of Ralph Twitchell to open his own architectural office in Sarasota. Born in Mansfield, Ohio, to a family who espoused going beyond the conventional, Twitchell had been encouraged to transfer from McGill to Columbia University, where there was a better architectural school curriculum. When World War I arrived, in a state of patriotic fervor he and a group of his college fraternity brothers volunteered for the Balloon Corps, leading eventually to his becoming a U.S. Air Corps pilot. With his characteristic desire to break barriers and "push the edge," Twitchell volunteered to be a test pilot (figure 2.16). His insatiable interest in stretching the limits nearly became fatal in a French air crash. But he survived, and on discharge he soon transferred his experimentalism to the practice of architecture. A courtly gentlemen, Twitchell immediately gained the confidence of the Sarasota art community with his firm's design and construction of a single-story gable-roofed, cypress-sided residence for author McKinlay Kantor in 1937 (figure 2.17).

2.16 | **Lieutenant Ralph Twitchell,** France, 1918

2.17 | **Kantor residence design drawing,** Sarasota, 1937; Ralph Twitchell, architect

2.18   **Corey Ford residence,** Freedom, New Hampshire, 1935; Ralph Twitchell, architect

From his earlier Sarasota stay, Twitchell remembered the special magic of its water-lined environment with tropical skies, unique light, beaches, surf, and islands imbued with exotic plants, trees, and creatures. Quick to see that seasonal Sarasota could not yet support a full-time architect, Twitchell formed a companion group called Associated Builders, Inc., to construct his architectural projects. In this way, he collected both the architect's and the contractor's fees while insuring high-quality construction for each project he did. He was truly a master builder, as his New England projects of the early 1930s had already shown (figure 2.18). During this period George Fulton worked with Twitchell in his architectural office. Lu Andrews was hired as his secretary/bookkeeper in Sarasota.[9]

The second event was the 1938 *Time* magazine cover article on Frank Lloyd Wright and his best-known work, "Fallingwater," located in Bear Run, Pennsylvania (figure 2.19). This recognition soon led to Wright's association with Dr. Ludd Spivey, president of Florida Southern College, who commissioned Wright to design a campus of exposed poured concrete and masonry buildings for this college only 60 miles from Sarasota in Lakeland,

2.19   **Fallingwater,** Bear Run, Pennsylvania, 1937; Frank Lloyd Wright, architect

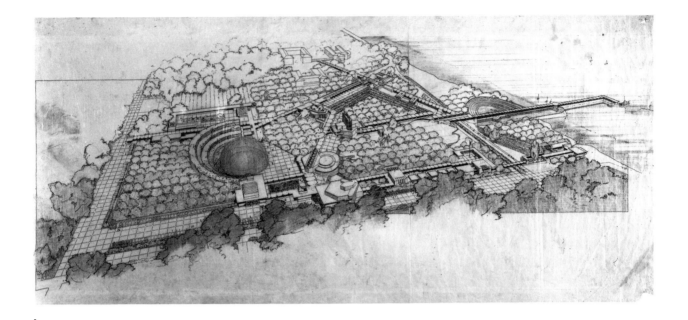

Florida Southern College aerial perspective, Lakeland, Florida, 1938; Frank Lloyd Wright, architect

Florida (figure 2.20). It is indeed ironic that the same Southern Methodists who earlier rejected Ringling's art school and museum now supported Wright's radical design. The project attracted national attention and the interest of the architectural profession in Florida.

All of this must have intrigued Ralph Twitchell, who had already worked in exposed natural stone, crafted sawn timbers, wood decking, and custom trim in his neoclassical residences before returning full time to Florida. Now with his new Sarasota construction company, he developed a residential concrete slab system on grade whose monolithic edges were turned down for footings on projects like the Kantor residence.[10] On this slab either masonry or wood-frame walls could be erected with French doors, fixed plate glass, and steel casement windows to fill in the openings. Corner casement windows were popular in conjunction with overhead corner roof cantilevers. Roofs were initially wood-gabled with overhangs. Finished exterior walls were either wood, stucco, or masonry. In 1938, Twitchell's interest in residential poured-concrete roof slabs led to his association with John Lambie to develop a metal form system for poured-concrete decks and walls. Out of this collaboration came, in 1939, a small, flat-roofed speculative Sarasota residence for Lu Andrews. It used Lambie's lamolithic system and spawned new ideas for the concrete construction of the Lido Beach Casino in 1940.

The WPA Lido Beach Casino project was announced in the *Sarasota Herald Tribune* on February 6, 1938, with Arthur Saxe as architect/engineer. For reasons no longer known the city council finally voted to give the project to Twitchell in March 1938, probably because of his stronger community and political ties (figure 2.21). Saxe was retained as a consultant on the job. With Phil Hammill now in his office, Twitchell reworked the elevations into the design that was built.[11] Hammill, who spent a great deal of time preparing the drawings for construction, was unfortunately drafted into the Army in late 1940 and did not see its completion.

Of reinforced concrete construction, the casino's most outstanding features were the precast items: the decorative cast concrete seahorses and the glass-block-and-concrete window frames set at 45 degrees to the building. The window units were described by Phil Hammill as a "diamond neck-lace" around the building. This glazing allowed filtered light into the public spaces by day and illuminated the outside perimeter by night. Flanked by two entry towers, the walled-in complex faced Lido Beach and the Gulf. Within was an Olympic-size swimming pool surrounded by cabanas, sun-bathing decks, locker rooms, shops, restaurants, lounges, and dancing areas. Its promenade on the water side provided access to the beach and the Gulf of Mexico. The main building had two stories, with a large second-level perimeter terrace and balcony for the band above the first-level res-taurant and dancing areas. The complex was to become a gathering place for Sarasotans for nearly three decades (figure 2.22).

Uneven in detail and quality of construction (like many WPA projects), the casino's design was frankly minimalist; concrete surfaces were left ex-posed, with thin roof slabs supported by poured beams on the top of the roofs, and long cantilevers exaggerated in places by a series of small deco-rative metal pipe column supports rather than one or two large support columns. The four towers were graceful and slim due to the structural co-herence of their verticals with the horizontal pipe handrails at the second level.

The Lido Beach Casino is now considered the bridge between Twitchell's work in the earlier 1930s and his pending total change to modernism. Sadly, this beach landmark was demolished in 1969 by the local politicians and businessmen who opposed the county-run facility.

Another Twitchell project, the 1938 Showboat House on Lake Louise, Flor-ida (figure 2.23), is set out over the lake on steel pipe columns resting on concrete piers and shows Twitchell's continuing innovation in construction details. By using steel beams combined with wood framing, Twitchell was able to create long open spans in the house inexpensively.

2.21 **Aerial view of Lido Beach Casino,** Siesta Key, 1940; Ralph Twitchell and Arthur Saxe, architects.

2.22 **Lido Beach Casino,** Siesta Key, 1940

2.23   **Showboat House,** Lake Louise, Florida, 1938; Ralph Twitchell, architect

2.24   **Second Lu Andrews residence,** Sarasota, 1940; Ralph Twitchell, architect

2.25 | **Rosenbaum residence,** Florence, Alabama, 1940; Frank Lloyd Wright, architect

Although Ralph Twitchell now resided in Sarasota, his family continued to alternate between Florida and New England. His office was much like a small atelier—he even had a cook/handyman on the premises. When the family was gone his several architectural and construction employees would periodically gather with him for supper and for a discussion of current events and architectural philosophy. A romanticist as well as a master builder, Twitchell and his group built a second house for Lu Andrews in 1940 (figure 2.24). It is their first-known stacked concrete block residence, with exterior upper plywood wall panels and a flat roof. The exterior was painted, the interior paneled in cypress. It bore a resemblance to Frank Lloyd Wrights' Usonian houses of the period; Twitchell, through his draftsmen, knew about Wright's 1939 Rosenbaum residence in Florence, Alabama (figure 2.25).[12]

By the end of 1940 Twitchell had moved from his early eclectic oeuvre to a consistent modernism. Along with his architectural studio and construction company, he began to assemble Sarasota waterfront property, with the idea of becoming a developer as well. The economy was improving, and prospects for building in Sarasota indeed looked promising for 1941.

CHAPTER THREE

THE AWAKENING: 1941–1946

In the spring of 1941 a young Alabama Polytechnic Institute graduate named Paul Rudolph sought and accepted employment in Ralph Twitchell's office (figure 3.1). Recommended to Twitchell by Phil Hammill, who had also attended API, Rudolph had been working for a Birmingham, Alabama, architectural firm since his graduation in 1940.[1] Enamored with Frank Lloyd Wright's recent work, particularly Florida Southern College, through architectural magazines, his architectural history courses, and word of mouth, Rudolph was attracted to tropical Florida (figure 3.2).

3.1   **Paul Rudolph, Steve Andrews, and Lu Andrews** at Florida Southern College, Lakeland, Florida, 1941

3.2   **Pfeiffer Chapel,** Florida Southern College, Lakeland, under construction, 1941; Frank Lloyd Wright, architect

3.3 **Fireplace bas reliefs,** Auburn, Alabama, 1940; Paul Rudolph, designer

3.4 **Futurama Exhibit,** a vision of the 1960s, at World's Fair, New York, 1939–1940

While at API his individual designs gained attention because of his rendering skills with Chinese ink on watercolor paper. Encouraged by the school's dean, Rudolph successfully applied to Harvard's Graduate School of Design.[2] His submittal to Harvard consisted of several larger API school projects done in gouache and photos of a small, nondescript, brick single-story house built for a professor at Auburn, Alabama. Inside, he had personally designed and fabricated the brick fireplace bas reliefs cut from Homasote that showed his creative potential (figure 3.3).

The son of a Methodist minister, Rudolph had early interests in music, sculpture, art, and architecture. He claims to have decided to become an architect at age seven or eight when he saw the drawings of a church addition for one of his father's congregations. In 1935 he entered the architecture program at API. In 1939 he visited Chicago, where he saw many of Frank Lloyd Wright's buildings, and the New York World's Fair, where he saw the contemporary fair buildings and exhibitions. The Futurama display there was likely Rudolph's first exposure to a vision of highrises and urbanism in architecture (figure 3.4).

In the short span of five Sarasota months, Twitchell's own residence and three others were designed with Rudolph's help and were under construction by Ed Root, his Associated Builders foreman. The first project was a small rectangular flat-roofed residence for Twitchell's in-laws, the Glor-

3.5 | **Glorieux residence,** Sarasota, 1941; Ralph Twitchell, architect

ieuxs (figure 3.5). Exquisitely detailed, this project represents Twitchell's first known use of Ocala limestone concrete block exposed inside and out. Its structural system of exposed cypress beams, four-by-four perlins, and homasote ceiling panels painted a blue-green set the direction for the next several projects.

Twitchell's residence at Big Pass, Siesta Key (figure 3.6), took more time to develop. Although Paul Rudolph claims no authorship in the basic design of this house, the finished work bears a distinct departure from the recent Twitchell designs. It was obvious that Twitchell and Rudolph worked well together and some aspects of the work showed Rudolph's hand. The bending of its plan between living and sleeping quarters to gain the panoramic Gulf view available and the use of angular motifs in its tapered structural members and decoration were entirely new ideas in Twitchell's work. The horizontal layering of various ceiling plane heights to differentiate service spaces from living spaces and the use of the strip windows were obviously derived from Wright. The large sliding-glass units framed in black cypress

3.6 **Twitchell residence,** Big Pass, Siesta Key, 1941–1942; Ralph Twitchell, architect

3.7 **Twitchell residence entry,** 1941–1942; door panels designed by Paul Rudolph

still exist in the house. The cut-wood front door panel designs and elongated cantilever entry beams appear to be Rudolph's contributions to the house (figure 3.7).[3] Despite having been remodeled, Twitchell's Big Pass residence remains today as his prewar residential classic.

The balance of the 1941 residences were either flat-roofed or slightly gabled, with beams and columns made up of spaced two-by-six wood members, broad overhangs, stacked exposed Ocala block walls, exposed horizontal battened wood wall siding, and large plate-glass window panels (figure 3.8). The designs echoed the horizontality of the flat Florida landscape. Entrances to these residences were often next to covered carports and the house proper was visually screened from the road by small outbuildings and walls. They were distinctively Florida designs and as such were attractive to second-home owners who came from more formal permanent out-of-state homes.

A final gable-roofed residence-studio in this manner was done for Kate Wheelan (figure 3.9). Asked by Mrs. Wheelan, a close friend of his family, in 1941 if he could possibly complete a residence with war imminent, Twitchell assured her that he could.[4] It is purported to have been built quickly while Twitchell was completing the design, and his ability to ferret out hard-to-get materials and equipment to finish it was amazing. This structure has since been demolished.

In the fall of 1941, Rudolph left Sarasota to enter Harvard Graduate School of Design, and the Twitchells moved into their nearly finished Big Pass house on December 1. On December 7, Pearl Harbor was attacked by the Japanese and the United States was officially at war. With no new work available, and his personal residence complete, Twitchell closed both his architectural and construction firms, and applied to reenlist in the air force. He was accepted to serve in early 1942.

3.10   **Lieutenant Paul Rudolph,** 1943

On completing his first year at Harvard in June, 1942, Rudolph enlisted in the U.S. Naval Reserve and began officer's training at MIT, finishing at Princeton (figure 3.10). The initial Harvard year had been an eye-opener for this young Alabama architectural graduate. His design class was personally taught by Walter Gropius, and among the students in his class was 35-year-old Phillip Johnson. The spread of war in Europe sent many eminent architects, designers, artists and scholars to the United States. Notable among the architects were Mies Van der Rohe, who settled at the Illinois Institute of Technology, and Walter Gropius with Marcel Breuer at Harvard. Rudolph was thus exposed to many world personalities in philosophy and the arts at the university.[5] He and his classmates made trips to Manhattan to visit museums, view architecture, and attend Broadway plays during the school year. Rudolph quickly recognized the importance of architects and other personalities in the arts as shown in his November 1941 letter to Lu Andrews (Ralph Twitchell's secretary from 1936 to 1941): "Last Friday he [Walter Gropius] had us out for cocktails at his famous home [figure 3.11]. There was a butler and his famous actress wife. She was truly charming and flirted with all of us."[6]

This house was in many ways a summation of Gropius's ideas taken from the earlier German Bauhaus school combined with his response to the American environment. Set on a Massachusetts hill, its flat roof, spare white walls, and sheer glass windows contrasted with heavier stone-walled, gabled, and hipped-roof neighbors. Inside, all was shades of white

with cork tile floors, accessories, and furniture designed by Marcel Breuer. Lightness and freedom from tradition were its hallmarks. Team design, consisting of Gropius and Breuer's joint efforts in this case, was Gropius's method of creating architecture. Gropius's philosophy was to have a profound effect on Rudolph and many other Harvard graduates during his tenure there.

Meanwhile, Colonel Ralph Twitchell was made group commander at the Charleston, South Carolina, Air Force Base in 1942. His position enabled him to keep in touch with Sarasota by occasionally flying back and forth to Sarasota's air base on "training missions." During his absence, Roberta Finney acted as his temporary Sarasota business manager.

Other future Sarasota contemporaries at different locales were also affected by the war. Jack West, who would become Twitchell and Rudolph's first employee in 1949, entered the navy from the University of Illinois.

Mark Hampton, who became Twitchell and Rudolph's second employee in 1950, joined the army through his ROTC program at the Georgia Institute of Technology. Victor Lundy, while attending architectural school at City College of New York, was drafted by the U.S. Army at age 19. Gene Leedy, the youngest of the future Sarasota group at age 15, had completed Florida secondary schools and soon entered the University of Florida.

In Sarasota, the tourists were replaced by thousands of servicemen who trained at the WPA-built Sarasota-Bradenton Air Field as fighter and bomber pilots. Servicemen on leave from their Tampa, Arcadia, and Venice, Florida, training bases also came to Sarasota's gulf beaches, attractions, and nightclubs.

By 1944, Ralph Twitchell had been transferred to the Columbia, South Carolina, Air Force Base as its commander. Lieutenant Paul Rudolph was officer-in-charge of navy ship construction at the Brooklyn Naval Yard. Here he learned the intricacies of coordinating men and materials in heavy industry.[7]

Lundy, Hampton, and West were exposed to overseas combat. Lundy (figure 3.12), awarded the Purple Heart for being wounded in action, recorded his European war experience in sketchbooks he later used to successfully apply for his Rotch traveling fellowship at Harvard in 1948 (figure 3.13).

3.12   **Sergeant Victor Lundy,** 1944

The response of the group to the war was a straight-arrow, get-it-done attitude. With the exception of the younger Leedy, they were soon to be part of what was to be called the G.I. generation. There was a great sense of trust and peer discipline among themselves. Full of optimism for the future, they were quick to return to work or school once the war was over, eager to make their architectural mark on the world.

Bourg de Lestre
Sept. 19, 1944

GERMAN PATROL
TOOK WARSHBERG NOV. 1, 1944

"PAT" (T/SGT. FAIENRUD)
ZEROING IN WITH THE 60 MM MORTARS
IN FRONT OF THE 3RD PLATOON.

Sept. 21, 1944
Bourg de Lestre

Part of the Atlantic Wall
6 men from L Co. hurt here
6 killed

Sept. 21, 1944

Quineville

NOV. 1, 1944

ONE OF THE 4-MEN GERMAN PATROL
WHO DIDN'T GET BACK.

CHAPTER FOUR

THE BEGINNING: 1946–1948

At the end of the war, Ralph Twitchell, discharged early from the air force, returned to Sarasota in 1945. There he built a new exposed block, glass and wood studio/residence for himself on Siesta Key. Since demolished, this project appears to have been totally designed by Twitchell (figure 4.1).[1]

Twitchell and Paul Rudolph had kept in touch during the war. On reviewing their highly successful 1941 collaboration, Twitchell again offered Rudolph a position and offered Jack Twitchell, his nephew, the charge of the construction company, Associated Builders. Both accepted. According to Jack Twitchell, Ralph Twitchell saw that he himself had the builder's skills and client contacts, while Rudolph had the designer's eye and rendering skills. Jack Twitchell, with his uncle's interest in detailing, would be able to carry out and complete their projects. It appeared to be the perfect marriage of talents.

Rudolph, discharged from the navy in 1946, returned to his last graduate year at Harvard. While stationed in New York he had the opportunity to become thoroughly acquainted with the Museum of Modern Art and its staff. He viewed the 1944 "Built in the U.S.A." architectural exhibit, and 1946 brought MOMA exhibits of Charles Eames's contemporary molded plywood chairs and of Mies Van der Rohe's work.[2] In what spare time he had, Rudolph began experimenting with new techniques in ink rendering.[3]

4.1 **Twitchell studio-residence elevation,** Big Pass, Siesta Key, 1945; Ralph Twitchell, architect

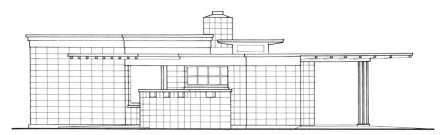

Between school terms, Rudolph was again in Twitchell's office to help design a cypress-post-and-beam residence for Merian Miller, planned in the shape of a **T**. The smaller bedrooms on the stem of the **T** were reached by a roofed outdoor walkway. It consisted of floor-to-ceiling glass walls, flat roofs, and exposed stacked lime block—by now a Twitchell trademark. Rudolph prepared black-and-white ink renderings of the design on gray illustration board that were widely published in 1948 (figure 4.2).

4.2 | **Miller residence,** Casey Key, 1947;

Ralph Twitchell, architect, Paul Rudolph, associate

4.3 | **Miller guest cottage,** Casey Key, 1947;

Ralph Twitchell, architect, Paul Rudolph, associate

The next Merian Miller project, in 1946, was a small wood-frame guest cottage on the same property (figure 4.3). Raised above grade on Casey Key and jutting into the water, it was a definite break from the 1941 projects, yet it bore a relationship to Twitchell's 1938 Showboat House on Lake Louise (figure 4.4).

4.4 **Showboat House,** Lake Louise, Florida, 1938;

Ralph Twitchell, architect

The Miller cottage was a flat-roofed, nearly one-room, post-and-beam wood-frame structure with the kitchen-bath area separated by a metal fireplace hood. The main space was expanded by floor-to-ceiling glass to a wood deck and a view of the water. The exterior was trimmed in bleached gray vertical cypress siding with high fixed windows for privacy from the road side. Slim casement windows were used for ventilation. Its structure lightly "hovered over" compared to the earlier Showboat House which literally "floated in" the water. The larger two-story Showboat House was nautical in theme with its round porthole windows and its curved bow of glass windows. The exterior walls of horizontal wood siding were painted white, creating a streamlined appearance. In contrast, the spareness of the Miller Cottage, cantilevered on either side, nearly relieved it of any sense of weight or gravity.

At the same time, a large winter vacation home on the Gulf was designed for a Mrs. Denman who frequently entertained. A **U**-shaped plan was devised that separated the service/living areas and the bedroom wing with a connecting sunroom (figure 4.5). The cypress post-and-beam structure was consciously exposed to make the purpose of each member or element immediately apparent. "Honesty of materials" was a term Twitchell and Rudolph often used to described their early projects.[4]

Twitchell and Rudolph found that their different attitudes complemented each other.[5] While Twitchell was quietly confident, Rudolph was ambitiously aggressive; while Twitchell was content to stay in Sarasota, Rudolph felt somewhat limited by the confines of Sarasota and Florida. Probably their age difference—Twitchell was 28 years older than Rudolph—

accounted for some of the contrast between the two. Twitchell was father and teacher at this time. The common bond between them was their similar educational experiences, strengthened by their mutual willingness to explore and try new ideas. Their differences became their strengths.

Another project designed in 1947 (built in 1948) was the rectangular Sarasota studio for Twitchell and Rudolph's earliest architectural photographer, Joseph Steinmetz. Steinmetz, who was with *Life* magazine, had a state-of-the-art darkroom done for him, complete with an early through-the-wall air-conditioning unit. The studio was constructed with exposed four-by-eight posts sandwiched between wood beams with stacked block and high glass window bands. The main building was set back from the street, its wood beams extended over the sidewalk to support a roofed canopy running parallel to the street. This unique urban gesture to make the public at one with the building sheltered passersby as roof canopies and marquees did on downtown Sarasota sidewalks. The structure still exists, with an enclosing masonry wall added in recent years (figure 4.6).

4.6 **Steinmetz studio,** Sarasota, 1947–1948; Ralph Twitchell, architect, Paul Rudolph, associate

4.7 Lucienne Twitchell residence,

Martha's Vineyard, Massachusetts, 1947–1951;

Twitchell and Rudolph, architects

Twitchell and his first wife, Lucienne, were divorced at the end of the war.[6] Her parents maintained a Manhattan brownstone in addition to their Sarasota residence. At this time, Lucienne, who spent part of her time in New York, asked Rudolph to help design a residence in Martha's Vineyard for her after finishing at Harvard (figure 4.7). Similar in appearance to the Miller Cottage on Siesta Key, the project was built later (1951). During construction by the two Twitchell sons, lateral stiffness problems developed which the senior Twitchells (Ralph and Jack) were able to solve from Florida.[7] Unfortunately, this house was later destroyed by fire.

Upon Rudolph's graduation from Harvard in 1947, he was awarded the Wheelwright Scholarship for travel in Europe. Apparently the trip was taken from mid-1948 to mid-1949. There he became familiar with Le Corbusier's built work. From visiting the older European towns and cities he learned the importance of urban planning.[8] Before Europe, Twitchell offered him a full partnership, which he accepted.

During Rudolph's Harvard and European sojourns, he experimented with ideas that were unique to the Florida climate. For a site on Siesta Key he conceived a project that was truly visionary: the Finney residence and guest house connected by a wooden walkway over a lagoon (figure 4.8). Lightly perched on the flat Florida landscape with the infinite horizontal of the Gulf of Mexico in view, this project was prophetic of what Florida was to come with the Kennedy Space Center in the 1960s.

As designed, the Finney residence lagoon artificially cut through and under the wood-frame structure. The building itself was cut into, and views from within were directed out by walls riding under the beam structural system and by changes in the raised platform levels. The dramatic entry boardwalk and wall seem to extend past the house into the infinity of the Gulf. Angularity—recalled from Twitchell's original 1942 residence—is seen in the structure and a new idea is introduced: great slatted storm shutters for both hurricane and shade protection. These lift-up panels were often pro-

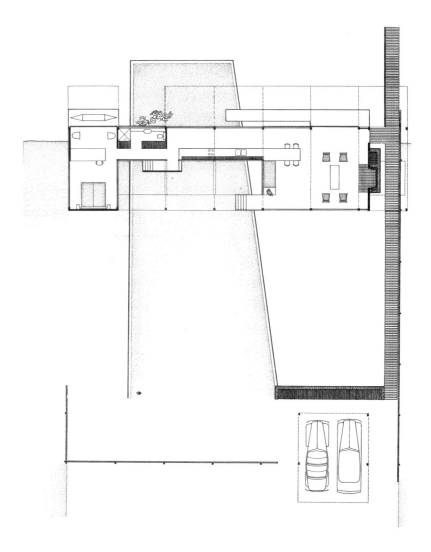

4.8 **Finney residence and guest house,** Siesta Key, 1947 (unbuilt); Ralph Twitchell, architect, Paul Rudolph, associate (renderings by Paul Rudolph)

posed in the firm's future designs. Rudolph's pen-and-ink talent had matured with the Finney project, and although it was never built, his drawings, widely published, greatly enhanced the reputation of the new partnership. Publication of this project soon proved to be the early turning point in their postwar careers.

CHAPTER FIVE

RECOGNITION: 1948–1950

Spaced between Sarasota projects were Rudolph's visits to New York to make contact with colleagues and the architectural periodicals there. Through *Architectural Forum* and his New York connections, the partnership was recommended to do a Florida house sponsored by the Revere Copper Company. Roberta Finney was the client. Most of the construction drawings were prepared in New York by Rudolph in early 1948. Twitchell's prewar experience with John Lambie's concrete system was utilized in the project. The house consisted of a flat roof-plane of concrete set on perimeter steel lally columns, similar to Mies van der Rohe's Barcelona pavilion concept of 1929. This allowed interior partitions to be placed anywhere. The non-loadbearing exterior walls were also of poured concrete (figure 5.1). During the early design phase, Rudolph proposed a grouping of six residences interconnected and divided by six-foot-high walls on the site (figure 5.2). This urban plan gave way to the more popular suburban one-house-to-one-lot concept they built.

5.1   **Revere house,** Siesta Key, 1948; Twitchell and Rudolph, architects

With the Revere house, Twitchell and Rudolph established the model for the classic 1950s Florida residence: a narrow one-story rectangle, often one room wide for cross-ventilation from glass jalousie windows; slab on grade; terrazzo floors; non-loadbearing walls with high glass window bands; wide overhangs, top-lit interior courts; and attached service buildings or carports, often connected by screen walls to the residence. To achieve the thin ceiling planes in the Revere house, it was necessary to pour a roof slab with beams on top whose surface accommodated ponds of water to help insulate the house. The use of a copper-sheathed fireplace hood and kitchen vent tied it to the Revere Copper Company advertising promotions of 1948 (figure 5.3).

5.2 | **Aerial view of six residences proposed for Revere property,** Siesta Key, 1948

(not built; rendering by Paul Rudolph)

5.3 | **Revere house,** courtyard

The Revere house was opened to the public in late 1948 and over 16,000 people visited the project in its first year. By now, Rudolph, who had made his first public speech at the Ringling Museum, was in demand as guest lecturer and critic at various schools of architecture. His home remained in Sarasota with Twitchell, while he periodically broadened their base of influence elsewhere. Rudolph's awareness that architectural and shelter journals were newsmagazines with great opportunities for publicity was put to good use with his exquisite ink renderings, an eye for newsworthy angles for projects, and collaboration with one of the postwar period's best architectural photographers, Ezra Stoller.

During his European trip, Rudolph made contact with the French architectural magazine *L'Architecture d'aujourd'hui* in 1949. He was selected by the magazine to collect and edit background material on Walter Gropius's Harvard years. Done as an assemblage of Harvard student and postgraduate architectural work in the U.S. honoring Gropius, the resultant February, 1950, article, entitled "Walter Gropius—the Spread of an Idea," recognized Gropius's American presence but showed his students as new individual modernists, moving away from his collaborative Bauhaus philosophy.

At the same time as the Revere house was built, four poured-in-place concrete homes were designed by Twitchell and Rudolph on Siesta Key for John Lambie, who was both contractor and developer of the project. In spite of Twitchell's earlier success with concrete, this project and the Revere house proved to be very expensive to build in the Florida economy, and from that point on a more economical wood and light steel framing system was utilized for Twitchell-Rudolph residential projects.[1]

An outgrowth of the earlier Finney design concept was the Siegriest residence, built in Venice, Florida, in 1949 (figure 5.4). Composed of sloping modular wood beam and roof deck members, the grouping of its several elements—screened toplit porch, patio, and carport—sprang from the main house and was visually held together by a common wood valence and privacy walls. It was part of the Museum of Modern Art's "Made in USA" exhibition on postwar architecture in 1950.

Because their design ideas often seemed radical to clients, Ralph Twitchell built some of their early projects for family or employees. The most notable was a project for Twitchell's new in-laws, the Healys.[2] It was a small guest cottage based on technological ideas he and Rudolph had gained from their World War II experiences. Again, it was a single-story rectangle with its platform floor lifted above grade and extended into the adjacent lagoon.

5.4   **Siegriest residence,** Venice, Florida 1949; Twitchell and Rudolph, architects

5.5   **Healy "Cocoon House,"** Siesta Key, under construction, 1950;

Twitchell and Rudolph, architects

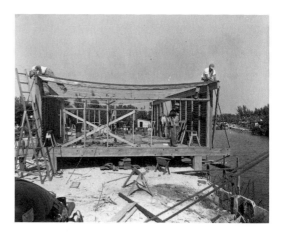

What was unusual was its inverted curved catenary roof. It was made by first installing the braced columns and beams with the platform. Then thin steel straps were individually draped across and welded to steel fascia angles attached to the perimeter roof beams on each side (figure 5.5). Once this was complete, flexible ceiling-insulation panels were installed on the straps, conforming to the curve, and sprayed with a special saran-vinyl plastic roofing material used to "mothball" U.S. Navy ships after the war. Called the "Cocoon House," its revolutionary concept captured international attention.

Concerned about the stiffness of the end glass walls, Twitchell-Rudolph devised a simple trussed tension unit to fit in the exterior horizontal wood valance (figure 5.6). It proved unnecessary, because once the fixed glass sheet was securely attached to its perimeter frame it stiffened the total structure sufficiently. Afterward, more than one contractor complained about structural vibrations in the beginning of their constructions for Twitchell-Rudolph's work. From his Cocoon House experience Rudolph would confidently dismiss their comments with, "The glass will stiffen it up." [3]

Fame was not without its problems. Initially there was criticism that the catenary structure was better suited to a larger-scale building situation. Rudolph responded that he couldn't wait. Because much of their design was experimental, some of their details did not always work as expected. It was then up to their in-house contractor, Jack Twitchell, to find an acceptable solution to the problem. Such was the case with the sprayed-on plastic roof film of the Cocoon House, the skin of which easily punctured and leaked. A more reliable, less aesthetic, built-up roof was finally applied over the surface. Another design item, its sculptural metal freestanding fireplace, never quite worked. Fortunately the Cocoon House was restored in 1990, and it proudly stands today as a classic 1950s Florida beach cottage.

5.6 | **Healy "Cocoon House,"** Siesta Key, 1948–1950 (rendering by Paul Rudolph)

In 1949, due to the heavy work loads of the two principals, Jack West was added to the firm soon after graduating from the Yale School of Architecture. Shortly after, Gene Leedy came to Sarasota to work for the Zimmermans, father and son architects who had originally come from Chicago in the 1940s. In 1950 Mark Hampton came to Twitchell-Rudolph to replace West, who left to start his own office. Prompted by these early architects' work here, critics such as Henry-Russell Hitchcock began to take notice of Sarasota architecture.[4] One by one, a group of adventuresome architects arrived, eager to explore the new creative edge.

The cooperation of Phil Hall, with his contemporary interior design studio and showroom, gave another dimension to the group's work. Since most of the built projects continued to be residential, the best way to ensure publication was to appropriately furnish each finished project for photographs. Usually the proud clients had spent every penny they had for the house proper, with no money left for furnishings. Fortunately, Phil Hall would oblige with a truckload of contemporary furniture, and the architect would arrive with the architectural photographer and complementary greenery. Once photographed, the furniture left the project and returned to Phil Hall's showroom for use another time.[5]

Ingenuity became a necessity for these architects, craftsmen, and builders to realize their one-of-a-kind, original creations. Jack Twitchell, as mentioned, was largely responsible for making a number of Twitchell-Rudolph experimental concepts work when constructed. Harold Pickett, a Sarasota contractor and inventor, developed a paper-honeycomb "plywood sandwich" panel that many of the architects used for the walls, beams, and roof systems of their projects in the 1950s. Woody White, a local glass contractor, answered the call for larger sliding glass doors by modifying the earlier wood-frame unit to a stronger, larger, extruded aluminum frame. In addition to his furniture showroom, Phil Hall, who was an industrial designer, created built-in furniture and cabinetwork for some of the projects.[6]

Because of Sarasota's small size, the few architects then living there tended to be friends and took an interest in each other's work without an ugly sense of competitiveness, according to Gene Leedy. Often several—Rudolph, Leedy, Hampton, West, Seibert, and later Rupp and Brosmith—would meet informally for lunch at the Plaza Restaurant in downtown Sarasota to comment on the day's happenings and to exchange ideas. This restaurant and bar was also the place where Sarasota's photographers, writers, and artists, such as Joseph Steinmetz, John McDonald, Syd Solomon, Ben Stahl, and Thornton Utz, met on a regular basis.[7]

In the short span of two years Twitchell and Rudolph had gained international recognition for Sarasota with a handful of small residences and guest cottages. With their projects they had given Sarasota and Florida an architectural identity of its own. The publicity attracted other interesting personalities to Sarasota. Among them were Philip Hiss, writer, developer, and patron, who was later to become County School Board chairman and founder of New College, and A. Everett "Chick" Austin, who became the director of the Ringling Museum when it was finally opened to the public as a state institution. Postwar critical and design luminaries Henry-Russell Hitchcock, Alexander Girard, George Nelson, and Charles and Ray Eames visited Sarasota to observe what was going on.[8]

It was a heady, expansive time for architecture in Sarasota and the early postwar period had been kind to the profession. The architects who were to form the Sarasota school came almost accidentally, without a preconceived plan or strategy. They had been attracted by Twitchell and Rudolph's work of the 1940s, which early embraced many of Frank Lloyd Wright's ideas. Reconstituted in 1949 by Rudolph after his Harvard, World War II, and European experiences, and with Ralph Twitchell's close support, their firm's work reached a new maturity of design by 1950.

CHAPTER SIX

THE GATHERING: THE 1950s

Twitchell and Rudolph's post–World War II successes and publicity drew not only visitors interested in their visionary configurations, but also new clients for their designs. Projects ranged from their first two-story residence, the Leavengood residence in St. Petersburg, to a redo of the Cocoon House idea in the form of catenary gabled roofs for Kate Wheelan's guest cottages and for the Coward residence (figure 6.1) on Siesta Key.

Much of their 1950–1951 work was a continuation of their single-story rectangular concept for domestic constructions. Buildings now became solids floating at the second-story level above their flat sites. The original Leavengood house rendering by Rudolph is an excellent example of this (figure 6.2). By raising the structure on columns, they caught more breeze, had a better view, and gained an economical shaded first level. Bedrooms were placed at the top, with the living, dining, kitchen, and court spaces on the ground level. The final Leavengood house sat more firmly on the ground and its design and detailing took a more Miesian approach (figure 6.3).[1]

At the same time, the Zimmermans designed and built several "South Seas" residential projects derived from their earlier experiences in the Pacific. These designs were one-story gable-roofed structures. In 1950 they hired Gene Leedy to develop a new architectural direction; he produced a more Floridian speculative house that emphasized horizontal lines (figure 6.4). In 1950, Phil Hiss designed and built his first two-story concrete "stilt" house directly on the water, encouraging further development directly on Sarasota Bay and Gulf of Mexico waterfront property (figure 6.5). Victor Lundy arrived from New York City to do a Sarasota home for Ben Stahl, a nationally known artist. Lundy's initial Sarasota trip would soon turn into a permanent stay.

One of Jack West's first projects on his own was a small contemporary cottage on Siesta Key (figure 6.6) for his mother, who wintered in Sarasota. Two-tiered for spatial interest and bedroom privacy, the flat-roofed structure was articulated with cypress boards framing the fixed glass and jalousie window units. The end walls were of windowless Ocala block to provide privacy from neighboring houses.

6.1   **Coward residence,** Siesta Key, 1950; Twitchell and Rudolph, architects

6.2   **Leavengood residence,** St. Petersburg, Florida, 1951; Twitchell and Rudolph, architects (rendering by Paul Rudolph)

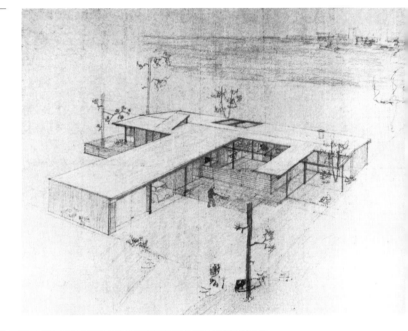

6.6 **Myrtle West residence,** Siesta Key, 1951; Jack West, architect

6.7 **Seibert residence,** Siesta Key, 1951–1952; Tim Seibert, architect

Tim Seibert, who has just completed architectural school, began construction of his first house, built by himself, in stages. The initial unit, next to a bayou with a boat dock, was constructed first. It was a basic post-and-beam rectangular box housing living, sleeping, kitchen, and bath (figure 6.7).

Later, a second unit with a bath and two bedrooms, identical in size, was added with perimeter walls linking the two, creating a pleasant beamed and screened courtyard between. Seibert, who has had several careers in Sarasota, worked briefly as a draftsman for Rudolph and for Philip Hiss, and as a carpenter for Jack Twitchell. He was also associated with his father, a retired navy engineer, before forming his own architectural firm.

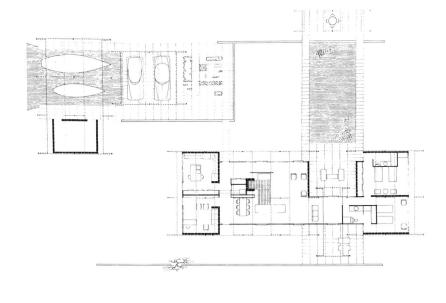

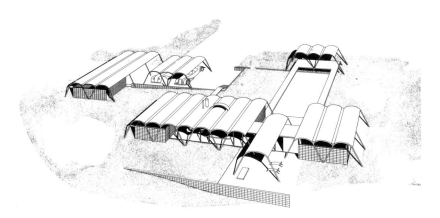

6.8 | **Knott residence 1,** Yankeetown, Florida, 1951–1952 (unbuilt); Paul Rudolph, architect

With more work available more architects arrived, but projects continued to be smaller residential and commercial buildings. This soon became an economic frustration for both Twitchell and Rudolph. Finally, in March 1951, the two principals dissolved their partnership and formed separate offices. Twitchell briefly retained Jack West and Rudolph soon hired Gene Leedy.

Sustained mainly by his college and speaking engagement income, Rudolph quickly pursued a new design direction with a new material: marine plywood. Molded into hulls for World War II PT boats, plywood was first used by Rudolph architecturally as roof vaults for the Knott residence, Yankeetown, Florida (figure 6.8), and the Hook residence, Siesta Key (figure 6.9). Extremely graceful, the vaults seemed to float over the flat Florida landscape. Unfortunately, Rudolph's vision exceeded technology in the case of the Knott residence. The thin vault edges of his highly publicized design lacked the structural rigidity necessary to support this roof. This design was never built. The problem was corrected in the case of Rudolph's Hook residence and the later Sanderling Beach Club (figure 6.10), Siesta Key, where heavier braced perimeter beam edges were used, as in the earlier Cocoon House.[2]

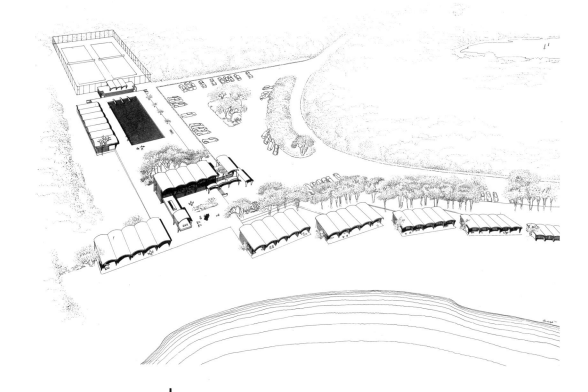

6.10   **Sanderling Beach Club,** Siesta Key, 1952; Paul Rudolph, architect

6.11   **Walker guest house,** Sanibel Island, Florida, 1952; Paul Rudolph, architect

Rudolph by now had his own individual presence in the architecture world. His first national commission after the breakup of the partnership was to design the Good Design Exhibition of 1952 installed at the Merchandise Mart, Chicago, and the Museum of Modern Art, New York. Another Florida project, the Walker guest house, Sanibel Island (figure 6.11), was built at the same time using movable plywood "flaps" within its wooden eight-by-eight-foot grid framework. The perfect simplicity of its form on an isolated beach generates monumentality despite its tiny size of 24 feet square. Despite their ephemeral appearance, the flaps really worked. Concrete balls—cast from rubber beach balls—hung as counterweights from the wood outriggers. Paul Rudolph once described this as his own personal Florida favorite: "It crouches like a spider in the sand."[3]

With the increased public visibility, architectural activity continued to increase in Sarasota. Jack West, who had earlier left Twitchell's office to start his own, returned for a short partnership with Twitchell. This partnership's design approach was a Miesian method of grids, often enclosed by large screen porches. The second Knott residence (built) is a good example of this phase of Twitchell-West work. Gene Leedy, called from Rudolph's office in 1952 to serve in the Korean War, returned to Sarasota in 1954 to start his own office. His initial work was smaller-scale speculative local wood residences on concrete slabs, following the single-story one-room-wide, flat-root design direction (figure 6.12). Floor-to-ceiling fixed and sliding glass panels created a feeling of spaciousness, of bringing the outdoors in. In good weather the glass panels could be totally opened to screen perimeter walls at the overhang edges (figure 6.13). This later led to Leedy's more individual, precast, prestressed concrete residential designs after he moved his office to Winter Haven, Florida, in 1955. Mark Hampton left Twitchell and Rudolph's office in 1951 to return to his hometown of Tampa to start his own office (figure 6.14). He also introduced new elements into the design mix: cement brick walls and an increased focus on interior design. A representative example is his Laura Hampton residence in Tampa (figure 6.15).

6.12   **Residence built for speculation,** Sarasota, 1954; Gene Leedy, architect

6.13   **Cross-section through residence,** Sarasota, 1954; Gene Leedy, architect

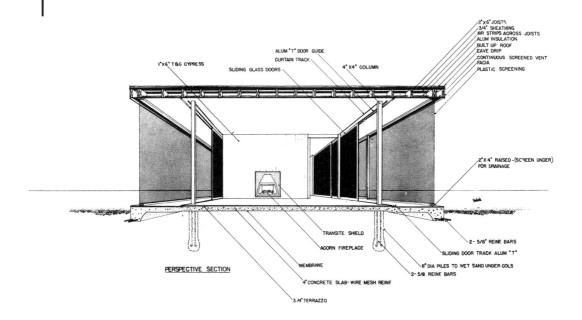

6.14 **Mark Hampton architectural office,** Tampa, 1953;

Mark Hampton, architect

6.15 **Laura Hampton residence,** Tampa, 1953;

Mark Hampton, architect

Meanwhile Rudolph continued to fuel the Sarasota image with his designs while balancing his local activities with frequent trips to his speaking and teaching assignments in the Northeast. A description by William Rupp of Rudolph's 1953 Florida office tells it all:

One bright June day in 1953 I disembarked from a Greyhound bus at the Sarasota station on Main street. Tired and seedy from two days of travel, much of it standing up, I walked directly across the street to 1644B to report to work. The luckiest young architectural graduate in the world, I had been called by Paul Rudolph to come work for him. I found a narrow dark arcade flanked by a barber shop and an upholstery shop. Second place on the left identified only by a card taped to the door, was my immediate future. When I entered a bespectacled young man looked up from a drawing board and said: "Paul is off to New York for a couple of days."

I started to work immediately relying only on a few written instructions left for me. This I found would be typical of the next two years.

We students at the University of Florida in the early 50's began to hear of an architect named Twitchell doing some remarkable work. Some students went down and reported that, in fact, the work was being done by a young Harvard man named Rudolph. Soon the publications were being sought and studied. A field trip was organized to see Frank Lloyd Wright's campus at Lakeland and over to Sarasota for the work of Twitchell and Rudolph. Both principals were out of town but an accommodating young man, Mark Hampton, their sole employee, took us on the tour. It is no understatement to say that we felt we had found "The Answer."

When making plans for graduation it became quite clear that the best possible experience would be to work for Rudolph. I wrote, but the reply was not very encouraging. A sudden reversal by telegram followed me to Philadelphia to which my father was returning after years in Florida. I called collect and was hired, assured that my pay would be $50 per week, extremely low even for that time and place. Later, I learned that the reversal was precipitated by the Fulbright Scholarship awarded to Bert Brosmith, who was slated to work there. The fact that I was chosen rather than one of the hundreds of other new graduates, was in part because I had office experience, partly by the recommendations of Sarasota friends.

Small in personnel, small in size (12' × 24'), it was rather well appointed, if crowded. The show window was screened with framed translucent plastic. Against the outside wall was a white painted steel framed sofa, with grey silk cover. This served as a bed for Rudolph's short stays. The longer stays he would find a place to rent.

Facing the sofa were two "British officer" chairs with canvas seats, backs and arms; hardwood legs. This chair was made famous by being used in many of Rudolph's drawings and published work. Behind the chairs partially screening the drawing tables, was suspended a large black & white blowup of a photo of a Rudolph building. Behind, four drawing tables crowded together were supported by crosslegged white painted steel horses. Both sidewalls were lined with shelves filled with books and journals. These were supported by white painted slender steel rods that reached to the gold teachest-papered ceiling and apparently supported a perforated screen that had been hand fabricated for the Good Design Exhibition of 1952 of the Museum of Modern Art, designed by Rudolph. This filtered the light from a skylight above. The steel columns supported showcase lamps for background light,

but the working light was by adjustable desk lamps. In the rear was a small lavatory, a shower, and

storage racks concealed by sliding plastic sheets. The floor was covered by grey sisal squares.

All white and grey, with a gold ceiling peeping through. How pure! "Pure" was a term that would be

bandied about a great deal in the future. Difficult to define; it generally meant some degree of perfec-

tion without pretense, either in form, structure, color or even purpose.[4]

6.16 | Phil Hiss

Rudolph's ability to come up with a fresh architectural encore continued with a significant new client, Philip Hiss, and his much-publicized project, the "Umbrella House." Hiss's community presence had become equal to the earlier influences of Mrs. Potter Palmer and the Ringlings. The son of a well-to-do doctor, Hiss inherited a considerable fortune at age 21 (figure 6.16). After touring the world by boat and motorcycle, writing a book on Bali, and completing a distinguished World War II career, Hiss made a sail-

6.17 **Hiss "umbrella" house,** Lido Shores, Florida, 1953; Paul Rudolph, architect

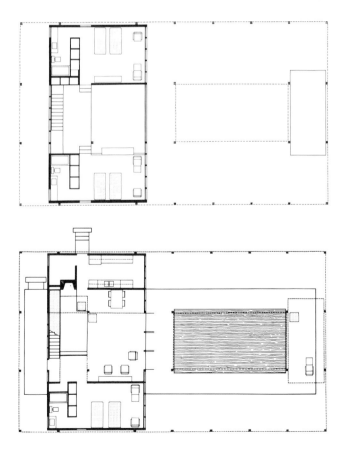

ing tour of the eastern United States coast and decided to settle in Sarasota. With his background as an anthropologist, writer, photographer, and developer (earlier in New Canaan, Connecticut), Hiss began to buy and develop waterfront property. He hired Paul Rudolph to design a speculative house for his Lido Shores development "to attract attention from the road and in the architectural journals," according to Bill Rupp. Hiss was not disappointed: the result was a very Floridian house of temple-like quality, with a high second wood-slat roof over the lower building masses for cooling and shading (figure 6.17). The house proper had two levels containing upper bedrooms at each end, with balconies and bridges over a two-story living-dining space that became a breezeway when opened. The slat roof continued out over a swimming pool and gazebo. Again, the structural so-

6.18 **Haywood Apartments, Sarasota,** 1953 (unbuilt); Paul Rudolph, architect

lution was difficult to attain, but it was ultimately successful and earned much publicity. The house's fragile lattice portion was eventually destroyed by a hurricane.

Between Florida projects, Rudolph found time to design Edward Steichen's "The Family of Man" exhibition for the Modern Museum of Art, with Bert Brosmith as project coordinator. In 1954, back in Florida, his work returned to more large two-story projects with his design of the Haywood Apartments in Sarasota (figure 6.18). This unbuilt project showed a freer interpretation of solids and voids within and without the upper umbrella-like flat slatted roof. The scheme embraced large open spaces visually protected by freestanding exterior wood screen walls. The plans, with semicircular walls and circular staircases, again showed the influence of Mies and Corb.

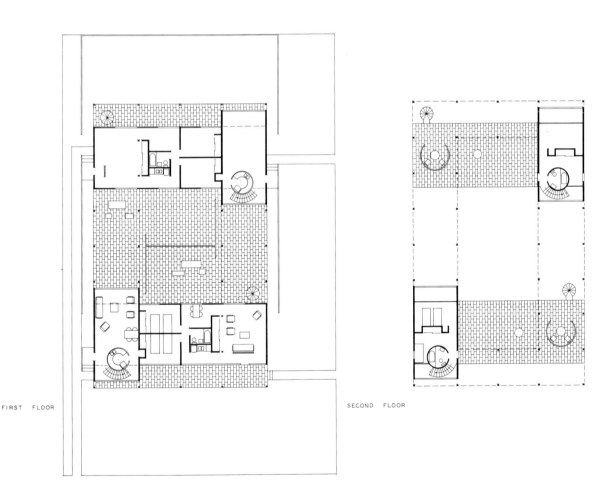

FIRST FLOOR

SECOND FLOOR

Awards and honors had become the norm for Sarasota architects by the mid-1950s. Rudolph was accorded the 1954 Young Architect's Award in São Paulo, Brazil (Gene Leedy's work was also displayed at the Brazil exhibition), and in 1955 Rudolph's Cohen residence garnered first design award out of 500 entries in *Progressive Architecture*'s second PA Awards Program (figure 6.20). The jury summary best characterizes the design of Rudolph (and the Sarasota group) as "work that represented actual and provable advance for 'Points of Departure' rather than mere competence or 'Points of Arrival.'"[5]

With this recognition, Rudolph firmly established himself as an important practitioner of modern American architecture and quieted some critics who had said his designs were too transitory and changeable. He was now recognized as having foreseen the formal vocabulary of the Space Age with his initial 1947 Finney residence of platforms over water (figure 6.21). His 1954 Cohen residence project (figure 6.22), with its spaceship-like multi-level structure, hovered over the Florida sand and mangroves. By using large, technologically available areas of glass with open voids, Rudolph was able to create a changeable architectural space inside and out as he had earlier done in the smaller Walker guest house. This two-story project was a nearly open-air pavilion with roofs, walls, and decks acting as large horizontal umbrellas. Through the use of hinged, movable wall panels the upper spaces could be totally enclosed or opened as the owner desired. With its winged walls open it gave the impression of instant takeoff into the sky. Below, a horizontal seawall with a deck extending over it from the house to the water was all that held the building to the ground.

In 1954, still another architect became a permanent part of the Sarasota legacy: Victor Lundy. Extremely talented and creative, Lundy was at Harvard while Rudolph was after the war, graduating two years after the latter. In many ways opposite to and competitive with Rudolph, Lundy brought a new approach to Sarasota. Born and raised on Manhattan's Upper East Side, Lundy was his high school's artist. At sixteen he enrolled in New York University. There he decided on architecture, and had begun the school's Beaux-Arts courses when he was drafted by the army in 1943. Coming from New York's man-made environment, Lundy discovered nature at Fort Jackson, South Carolina, before going overseas. His original talent in art showed in his wartime sketches, his work at Harvard and during his travelling fellowship, and finally in his Sarasota projects.

A colorist who could work in any artistic medium, Lundy felt out of place at Harvard, where most student work was done in black and white or shades of gray. After graduation and on his fellowship travels, he was repulsed by Corbusier's Paris studio and buildings. He decided to study and sketch European and north African historical buildings, which were more interesting to him.[6]

Once settled in Florida, Lundy made contact with the Sarasota art and religious communities. His first architectural project was a simple glass-and-wood flat-roofed building for a drive-in Presbyterian church in nearby Venice, Florida (since demolished). Basically it was a glass-enclosed elevated preaching platform, perched among tall pine trees and surrounded by parked parishioners at Sunday services. The idea and the building received national recognition in *Life*. The religious acknowledgement of an auto audience parked on grass was an instant link to Florida's tourist culture.

Attracting attention through his art displays (figure 6.23), Lundy was able to gain the commission for the new Chamber of Commerce building (figure 6.24).[7] It is essentially a glazed-tile-roofed pavilion with curved laminated wood beams, set on steel columns supporting its structural wood roof deck. Walls are glass panels. The building, still standing, sits in a garden bordering Sarasota Bay. Small, 30 by 80 feet, the building, with its air conditioned interior, was completed in 1956 for only $50,000.[8]

6.23   **Victor Lundy painting of his proposed Chamber of Commerce Building,** Sarasota, 1955

6.24   **Chamber of Commerce Building,** Sarasota, 1956; Victor Lundy, architect

6.25   **Bee Ridge Presbyterian Church,** Sarasota, 1956; Victor Lundy, architect

6.26   **Venice Presbyterian Church meeting hall,** Sarasota, 1956; Victor Lundy, architect

Curved laminated wood roof beams thrusting upward from the inside to the sky (or heavens) became a dominant theme for Lundy's churches in the 1950s and 1960s. Bee Ridge Presbyterian Church (figure 6.25) was the second of a remarkable group of almost lighter-than-air religious enclosures. Barely attached to earth with an occasional metal, stone, or concrete anchor, his system of shaped ribs started a roof structure which often ended with a light source (usually a skylight) at its peak.

The glass enclosure of his churches at ground level appeared almost as an afterthought. In the Venice Presbyterian Church meeting hall (figure 6.26), the large sliding glass doors were designed to be completely opened. While Gothic cathedrals achieved an uplifting lightness with a minimum of stone structure, Lundy's thin wooden skins seemed to skim the ground they sat on. With large overhangs, his work converted economic necessity into true spaciousness.

Where Rudolph's work in the 1940s began as an almost painful, methodical search of space and ended with the dissection and annihilation of the box, Lundy's work in the 1950s appeared suddenly, and seemingly effortlessly, to require as little material as possible to achieve his designs. With Lundy now in Sarasota, the two seemed to resume the competition begun at Harvard.

This appearance was deceptive, because once Rudolph achieved his own creative identity in 1947 his progress was lightning-quick. He jumped from one architectural concept to another, fired by his insatiable curiosity. Lundy, the younger by five years, had the advantage of viewing the post–World War II architectural groundwork of others, including Rudolph's work, as a vantage point for his own separate architectural growth. The fact that a tension did exist between the two contributed positive energy to the growth of the Sarasota group. Possibly their competition pushed each to a new level of achievement beyond which neither would have gone alone.

In 1956 Rudolph designed his first religious project (unbuilt): a sanctuary and Fellowship Hall for St. Boniface Episcopal Church, Siesta Key (figure 6.27). A new material—precast, prestressed reinforced concrete "T" units—was proposed for its sloping roof decks. What was unusual was that the T's were to be installed contrary to normal practice: with the stems of the T's on the top exposed to the outside, and the smooth side inside. The two sloped surfaces formed a gabled sanctuary roof and the exposed stem members overlapped the ridge to form alternating glass roof monitors on each ridge side, allowing light inside the sanctuary. Reversing the configuration of the tensile steel reinforcement made the roof structurally sound.

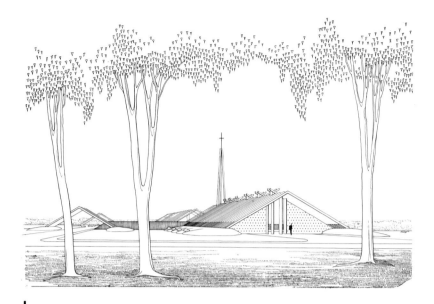

6.27   **St. Boniface Episcopal Church,** Siesta Key, 1956 (unbuilt); Paul Rudolph, architect

A year earlier Gene Leedy moved his office from Sarasota to Winter Haven, where he had been commissioned to do several residences. The most outgoing of the Sarasota group, he was also introspective and analytical. A promoter, he teamed up with a Winter Haven developer, Craney Homes, Inc., to produce the town's first enclave of contemporary homes (figure 6.28). Twelve were designed and built, closely following Leedy's designs.

Sales of the homes started slowly, and Leedy purchased one that he and his family continue to live in today (figure 6.29). Two rooms wide with a flat roof, its wood post-and-beam system supported four-inch-thick exposed wood decking. Sliding glass doors, jalousie windows, texture 1–11 plywood, and exposed concrete block walls completed the enclosure. Originally, five-foot-high wood screen walls visually separated each house and tied the complex together as a whole. The evolution of Leedy's thinking

6.28   **Site plan for Craney Homes,** Winter Haven, Florida, 1956;

Gene Leedy, architect

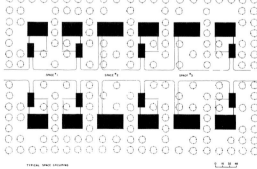

6.29   **Leedy residence,** Winter Haven, Florida, 1956; Gene Leedy, architect

6.30   **Leedy residence,** as later modified

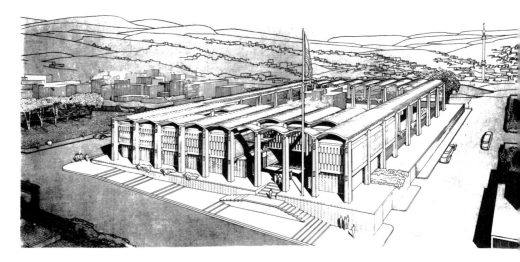

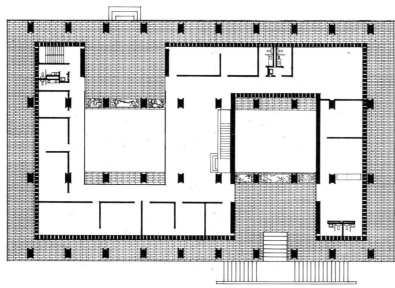

6.31 **U.S. Embassy,** Amman, Jordan, 1956; Paul Rudolph, architect

over the next two decades can be seen in the changes and additions he made to his residence and its neighbors (figure 6.30).

As Rudolph's reputation grew, he was awarded designing of the United States Embassy in Amman, Jordan, in 1956. for a hot, arid climate, the building he proposed had a canopy of concrete vaults over the lower buildings to shade and allow natural ventilation between the units (figure 6.31). The columns were made up of hollow masonry units to be filled with reinforced concrete. All sat on a masonry podium. Final construction drawings were done in 1956 but the project has never been built.

At the same time Sarasota began its innovative County School program, initiated by Philip Hiss after he was elected to the Board in 1954. Hiss demanded and was authorized to pick the best architects for new school buildings regardless of their experience. The new building program depended on the success of its first school project, Brookside Junior High School, awarded to Ralph and William Zimmerman. Before it was designed, a lengthy study was made of the existing Sarasota schools. They were found to be badly oriented, cold in the winter, hot in the summer, and poorly ventilated (economical air-conditioning was not yet available). They were overly institutional in appearance, their materials and equipment were of poor quality, and their maintenance costs were high.

The resultant Zimmerman school was an open plan (figure 6.32), and the structure was lightened with slim steel bents supporting four-inch wood decks. Jalousie windows were placed for natural ventilation, and large glass areas were used to bring in light. Lower covered walkway roofs also became overhangs for shading. Most important was the fact that the school's cost came in under budget, and Hiss's building program was assured acceptance by the Board and the community.

Thus a diverse group of Sarasota schools were designed and built between 1955 and 1959. Mark Hampton, with John Crowell as associate, designed Venice Junior High School (figure 6.33) in an H-shaped plan. Its structure was based on a three-foot module made up of round concrete columns supporting a two-way reinforced concrete waffle roof slab. Hampton also designed Amaryllis Park Elementary School (figure 6.34) which was an exposed black steel H column structure with concrete brick infill panels, glass and wood jalousie windows and glass sliding doors.

Gene Leedy, with William Rupp, designed Brentwood Elementary School (figure 6.35). Again, it was an exposed white painted steel-frame structure with brick walls, jalousie windows and sliding glass panel enclosures.

6.32 | **Brookside Junior High School,** Sarasota, 1956; Ralph and William Zimmerman, architects

6.33 | **Venice Junior High School,** 1957; Mark Hampton and John Crowell, associated architects

6.34 | **Amaryllis Park Elementary School,** Sarasota, 1959–1960; Mark Hampton, architect

6.35 | **Brentwood Elementary School,** Sarasota, 1958; Gene Leedy and William Rupp, associated architects

6.36 **Riverview Senior High School,** Sarasota, 1958–1959; Paul Rudolph, architect

6.37 **Alta Vista Elementary School addition,** Sarasota, 1958; Victor Lundy, architect

Paul Rudolph, Hiss's personal favorite architect, was awarded the largest project, Riverview Senior High School (figure 6.36). The complex was planned in the form of a two-story **U** focusing on a courtyard formed by its sides. Made up of exposed black painted steel columns and beams, the structure made a unique use of roofed monitor penthouses that periodically admitted controlled light to the double-loaded classroom walkways below. This alternating pattern was assisted by thin perimeter concrete canopy slab units, spaced top and bottom in horizontal steel frames, that allowed shade and airflow along the exterior glass walls. Again jalousie glass windows, fixed glass, sliding glass doors, and buff-colored concrete brick were utilized. Bert Brosmith, now in charge of Rudolph's Florida office, made major contributions to the detailing of this school. It is probably the most successful in terms of design and durability over the years of all the schools.

The smallest and most unusual of the new Sarasota schools was a soaring twelve-classroom addition to the existing Alta Vista Elementary School by Victor Lundy (figure 6.37). The wood-deck roof cover, similar in concept to his church roof, was conceived as a great freestanding shade shelter over the indoor-outdoor classrooms. Its eighteen-foot overhangs sheltered ample outdoor teaching spaces divided by brick walls. Solar heating was

used for the new hot-water system. Unfortunately, its double-loaded interior classroom corridor was covered with a glass skylight in an aluminum frame that did not always ventilate well, sometimes making conditions unbearable on hot or cold days. The wood-laminated wing-like structural bents supporting the structure's wood deck were held down by vertical steel rods near its ends. Aesthetically successful, its construction features have proved too temperamental for successful school maintenance.

The final school under Hiss's program, done in 1959, was the Sarasota Senior High School addition by Paul Rudolph, with Bert Brosmith as project architect (figure 6.38). Although Rudolph now was spending much time at Yale and in his Boston office, he was completely in control of the design. By now the influence of Le Corbusier's later work on Rudolph's work was very evident. The school's massive concrete volume opened and closed with carefully arranged horizontal concrete sunscreen panels that hung from its second-story concrete roof "ears." Exterior walls appeared from without to be mostly concrete frame or concrete brick. All concrete was finished white to repel the Florida heat.

Its exterior glass windows were shielded by these concrete solar panels held away from the building proper (figure 6.39). Inside, its double-loaded classroom corridors had spaced concrete roof monitors, again for controlled light as in Riverview High School. Future air-conditioning was to be installed in plenum spaces designed over the classrooms. Outside, covered walkways were white concrete, thin slab modular units reminiscent of Frank Lloyd Wright's segmented covered walkway at "Fallingwater." For all their weight, they lightly paraded in and out of the new addition and barely connected it to the adjacent two-story brick-and-terra-cotta 1920s high school. Due to its careful location to the side and behind the original school, Rudolph's work is comfortable with its older neighbor. Unfortunately, the harsh intrusion of a large asphalt parking lot connecting the two largely destroyed this balance.

Like the nine other schools, the Sarasota Senior High School addition looked so different that adverse reactions began to be heard from the public, the politicians, and the local newspapers. Phil Hiss's autocratic response to the criticism did not help.[9] Rudolph's concrete structure began to develop minor cracks, water leaks, and some differential settlement that later proved to be negligible. Sadly, Rudolph's last Sarasota school project became a symbol for the rejection of the Sarasota group's work, as local architects became less and less trusted to do such large works.

In retrospect, Hiss's program established new concepts and standards for postwar American secondary school planning and attracted international attention and interest. Classrooms were larger, more flexible spaces with

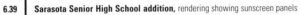

6.38 **Sarasota Senior High School addition,** 1959–1960; Paul Rudolph, architect

6.39 **Sarasota Senior High School addition,** rendering showing sunscreen panels

fewer students, providing the opportunity to teach more programs and more varied ones. Team teaching was introduced in two of the schools. Connected indoor and outdoor classroom spaces worked well in the Florida climate. Although set up for natural ventilation, many of the schools had provided space for future air-conditioning. Items such as built-in conduits for closed-circuit television and daylight screens for audiovisual programs were included. Overall, the county school program that developed new teaching and architectural concepts was a success.

Individually, other Sarasota school architects continued to receive notice for their work in and out of Sarasota. Mark Hampton's Jordan residence in Lake Wales (figure 6.40) received the 1957 Homes for Better Living Award sponsored by *Time, House and Home* and the American Institute of Architects. A larger project, the Galloway's Furniture showroom in Tampa, was Hampton's version of a rectangular Miesian glass enclosure (figure 6.41). Concurrently, Victor Lundy designed Galloway's Sarasota showroom (figure 6.42). An unusual circular building, its wood roof skin grew out of its center like a flower and expanded over its second-story balcony. Perimeter glass completed the enclosure. Lundy's motel for Warm Mineral Springs explored the use of precast concrete "mushroom" roof units set at alternating levels, enclosed with plexiglass panels, sliding glass doors and concrete-block walls (figure 6.43).

Probably the most complete group of Lundy's Florida buildings is at St. Paul's Lutheran Church, Sarasota (figure 6.44). Begun in 1958, the parish hall is a sweeping roof set on interlacing wood laminated beams. Supports are concrete piers. While the parish hall "extroverts" its space to the outside, the later church sanctuary compresses or "introverts" its space to focus on the pulpit. Here the curved wood roof is supported by a series of draped steel cables hanging in catenary curves from its ridge. The ridge is made up of steel triangular top members tied into the cables. Slits of light penetrate its lower concrete perimeter walls to silhouette its enclosure.

As the home of many of America's best architects, Sarasota gave them early recognition, then later chose to ignore them. Pressed by outside developers with unlimited funds, Sarasota County got state approval to sell its public beaches and recreational areas to these developers starting in 1956.[10] Thus began a series of community and political moves that fragmented Sarasota's land resources and negated any logical planning for the area. Rather than face these problems, Paul Rudolph had accepted the chairmanship of the Department of Architecture at Yale and Victor Lundy had started his second office in New York by 1960. However, the order, logic, and legacy of their architecture and ideas stayed in Sarasota.

6.40 | **Jordan residence,** Lake Wales, Florida, 1956; Mark Hampton, architect

6.42   **Galloway's Furniture showroom,** Sarasota, 1959;

Victor Lundy, architect

6.43   **Warm Mineral Springs Motel,** Venice, Florida, 1958;

Victor Lundy, architect

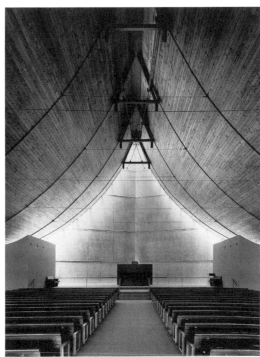

6.44 **St. Paul's Lutheran Church,** Sarasota, 1958–1970;

Victor Lundy, architect

CHAPTER SEVEN

NEW DIRECTIONS AND DECLINE: THE 1960s

In 1960, after Rudolph moved to Yale, Bert Brosmith closed down Rudolph's local office and began his own practice in Sarasota. Brosmith's first project was the Peter Hart island cottage in Naples (figure 7.1). Designed in a cruciform plan, the building's living, sleeping, and porch spaces were set above an open entrance podium elevated over grade. Its height afforded views in all four directions and the spaces could be opened up as one large screened unit in good weather.

Brosmith received a number of remodeling and addition projects through his relationship with Rudolph. His first larger project came from Philip Hiss: the Sarasota Junior High School addition (figure 7.2).[1] In many ways his design was a summation of the ideas and lessons learned from the Sarasota school. Built in horizontal layers on terraced ground, the classroom units were sheltered by a continuous flat-roofed plenum above with generous overhangs over walkways. This upper service space accommodated functions such as natural ventilation and air-conditioning systems.

7.1 **Hart island cottage,** Naples, Florida, 1960; Bert Brosmith, architect

SECOND FLOOR

FIRST FLOOR

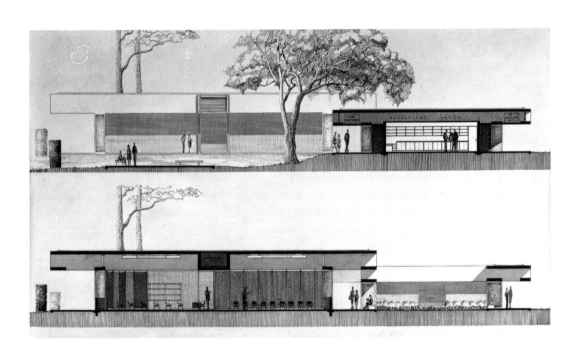

Sarasota Junior High School addition, 1961; Bert Brosmith, architect

7.3 | **Sarasota Senior High School addition,** 1959–1960, section perspective showing furture HVAC system; Paul Rudolph, architect

7.4 | **Leggitt residence site plan,** Tampa, Florida, 1959–1960; Paul Rudolph, architect

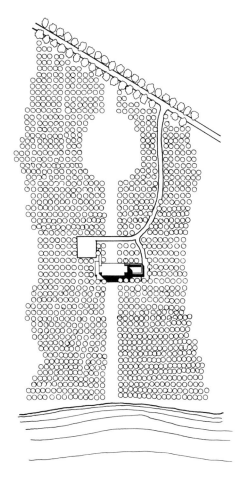

The combination of exposed concrete-block walls, glass, and steel-frame construction for economy produced a simpler design than those of the schools Brosmith had done under Rudolph in the 1950s. Up to this point, air-conditioning had not been an economic consideration. The earlier concrete Sarasota Senior High School buildings had space set aside for later air-conditioning machinery and ducts (figure 7.3). Unfortunately, neither Rudolph nor any of the other original school architects were later contacted by the School Board to complete the appropriate mechanical pathways for their schools when air-conditioning was added, and these later additions were aesthetically disastrous.[2]

During the transition from Rudolph's office to his own in 1959, Brosmith was involved with Rudolph in the two-story brick-walled and steel-framed Leggitt residence set in a mature grapefruit grove overlooking a lake in Tampa (figure 7.4). The power of scale is demonstrated here by resting the large residence at the high point of a visual swath cut through the large grove to the lake at its bottom. The Rudolph-designed house sat on a brick podium with paired rectangular brick columns that continue to give it scale at a distance. Elegant, with one-story brick-walled courtyards at its ends, it was a quiet combination of Rudolph's ideas and Brosmith's understanding and skillful execution of them.

A residence for the John Wallaces in Athens, Alabama (figure 7.5), was a more striking example of the principles Rudolph showed in the Leggitt residence. Again of dual columns—round columns of brick this time—its two-story combination of inner penetrating spaces under one roof was more open, with a dramatic curved staircase to upper levels. It was set on a brick podium surrounded by grass. All was painted white. Like a contemporary Greek temple, this design seemed to acknowledge the influence that Alabama Greek Revival architecture had on Rudolph during his student period there. Its large overhangs and balconies were appropriate to its Southern setting.

Although now removed from Florida, Rudolph demonstrated his continued knack for adapting his designs to their environmental location. His 1960 Milam residence in Jacksonville (figure 7.6), of exposed concrete block and poured concrete perimeters, was his sculptural response to the sun and views of northeast Florida. Facing the Atlantic Ocean from a sandy bluff, it has the feel both of Corb in its spaces and of Mondrian in its elaborate concrete screening "grille" on the oceanside.[3] It was a strong farewell to his Florida residential period in architecture.

A final southern residential project (unbuilt) for the Callahans of Birmingham, Alabama, became an even freer interpretation of Corb combined

7.5 **Wallace residence,** Athens, Alabama, 1961–1966;

Paul Rudolph, architect

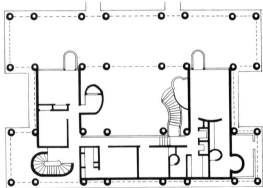

7.6 **Milam residence,** Jacksonville, Florida, 1960; Paul Rudolph, architect

with Rudolph's Florida trailer-module ideas (figure 7.7).[4] Again sitting on a podium, it juts out from a steeply sloping site. The interior spaces were expressed separately rather than as one mass. Arranged at the edges for sun and view control, its perimeter was similar to those of the Milam and earlier Bostwick residence (figure 7.8).

In Sarasota, Bert Brosmith's practice was becoming more varied with his commission for the Paulk Dental Office Building, composed of ordered rectangular concrete-block cubes carefully separated by vertical glass planes (figure 7.9). It is skillfully scaled to its surrounding neighbors even though only part of the planned complex was built.

7.7   **Callahan residence,** Birmingham, Alabama, 1965 (unbuilt); Paul Rudolph, architect

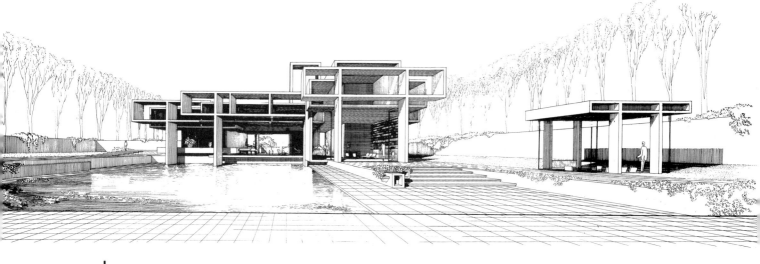

7.8 | **Bostwick residence,** Palm Beach, Florida, 1954 (unbuilt); Paul Rudolph, architect

7.9 | **Paulk Dental Office Building,** Sarasota, 1961; Bert Brosmith, architect

7.11   **McDonald residence,** Siesta Key, 1965; Tim Seibert, architect

The Zimmermans, flush from their successful county school projects, designed a more refined Polynesian-style residence—the Weaver beach house, Longboat Key—to add to their portfolio of tropical work (figure 7.10).

Tim Seibert, at this point in his career, established himself as the eclectic maverick of the group by exploring other architectural directions. His strong interest in historic Florida Cracker architecture resulted in a number of projects sympathetic to that style.[5] Author John D. MacDonald's residence on Siesta Key (figure 7.11) had a structural directness with its pressure-treated round wood poles set on concrete piles driven into the sand. Standard lumber beams, rafters, and perlins were bolted together and the hipped metal roof was directly screwed to the wood perlins. On the outside a raised broad porch on all four sides recognized the vernacular characteristic of early Florida homesteads. Inside, finishes and levels were more elaborate and contemporary, and the transparency of the large exterior glass walls clarify and emphasize the structural qualities of Florida Cracker architecture in this extensive beach house.

7.12   **Vacation house,** La Costa Island, Florida, 1964; Tim Seibert, architect

7.13   **Field Club,** Sarasota, 1961; Tim Seibert, architect

The purest Seibert Cracker project is a small vacation house on La Costa Island, Florida (figure 7.12). Essentially a hipped-roof, single-room structure again raised on wood poles, it sits gracefully on the beach dunes, its top-lit cupola allowing air circulation on hot days.

With the Field Club addition in 1961, Seibert showed his earlier modernist mode. Here he joined the existing 1920s stuccoed structure with a new transparent glass-enclosed dining room of multiple levels placed over a bayou. The transition from the heavy walls of the original building to the open, platformed expansion remains one of his most successful concepts (figure 7.13).

Although Victor Lundy now ran a second active office in New York, he maintained his Sarasota office with Boyd Blackner as project architect there. Blackner had come to Sarasota a year earlier (1959) at the urging of a friend and his description of Lundy's office bears repeating here:

We had just completed an exhausting, hot, long drive from Houston to Sarasota, and I just stopped by Victor Lundy's office to get oriented and say hello to Ron Cassetti, my former co-worker at Caudill Rowlett and Scott [well known Houston architects], who talked me into coming to work for Lundy. I hoped to get some suggestions on where to temporarily locate my wife and our two small children. Somehow, I had in my mind that we would get situated, unpack, and I would come to work in 3 or 4 days.

The office was on the third floor of a picturesque 1920's three story white, Mediterranean style stucco pile designed by Dwight James Baum, Florida West Coast's Addison Mizner, on First Street near the Tamiami Trail. A discreet polished brass plaque, "VICTOR A. LUNDY, ARCHITECT" identified an arch opening as the office entrance. Tile floors, white stucco walls, pre-Colombian art on pedestals, and a large, very sculptural, styrofoam screen carved by Lundy led up through a foyer, a curved staircase, and down a long hall. Where were the secretaries? Two doors. Voices. I knocked on one. It burst open with a flood of sunlight, disarray and confusion of ladders, mops, buckets, tables, models, rolls of drawings, photos, awards, certificates, and renderings to reveal Ron Cassetti and two other men. Before Ron could say anything to me the good looking, dark haired, powerfully built younger of the two said, "You must be Boyd! My God you're big! Can you draw?" Before I could answer he said, "Here, take this mop and bucket and swab out the hallway, stairs, and front foyer. The Atomic Energy

Commission is coming tomorrow for the interview. We have to find some people for the desks. Get a decent shirt for tomorrow! At least you're big!" This was my introduction to Victor Lundy.

Somehow, we did get settled. Vic got the A.E.C. job, and Ron confided "I hope we haven't made a mistake. There are urgent deadlines on four churches, a parsonage, two schools and a couple of houses and now we have this A.E.C. thing with just the three of us to do all the work." He meant Ed Kastner, a 60 year old career draftsman from Paducah, Kentucky, himself, and me. I was very relieved to hear Ed intone that "Vic may have his problems, but he's never missed a payroll!"

Victor worked in prodigious bursts—all night, weekends, in hotel rooms, and on planes. He produced superb, huge drawings, dripping with ink, water-color, oils, charcoal, crayon, pastels. Clay models that weighed 50 lbs. would emerge from his office on the other side of the hall. All these were true works of art that combined schematics, preliminaries and design development all into one plastiline phase. Also, there were sketch books filled with quotes from the client, impressions of the site, poetic searches for the essence of the project, design sketches, details, program areas and relationships, budget, schedules, calculations, specification items and instructions. He would even come in and letter finish schedules and title blocks late into the night if deadlines were really desperate.

The long theatrical trek from the entry to the offices was really to get to the top floor with its large, breezy, sun filled, jalousie windowed studio rooms overlooking Sarasota Bay. 1000H was the drafting medium (for the nice feel and tooth) at Lundy's with long, long T-squares on tables made from wood horses and flush wood doors. Without air conditioning, the drawings would grow and shrink during

the day depending on the morning fog, the afternoon rain, or the Florida sun. A set of ship's curves

was essential. Once I recovered from the Florida technology shock, I realized that this direct, passion-

ate, artist's atelier environment was an amazingly effective way to produce great architecture unen-

cumbered by large office politics and procedures.

Commissions, awards and recognition of national and international scope were flooding in. Lundy

established a New York office and thought nothing of flying me up to work on a project for a week

that would turn into a month. Ron Cassetti, Sandy Hirshen, Keith Kelly, Paul Losi, Richard Abbott,

Bob Greene, Jerry Thornton, and others shuttled between New York and Sarasota as well.

The Sarasota office was a magnet for editors, photographers, writers, and visiting architects from

around the world. Vic would say "Be nice to them but don't let them into the office where they can

interfere with the work or steal our ideas". Often, I became the "grip" or pack horse for photographers

from *Life, Time,* or *Look* or who were on assignment from the architectural press like Cserna, Georges,

Molitor, Shulman and others. We were proud of our batting average; that is, the ratio of the projects

awarded or published in relation to the volume of work. There was camaraderie within the office and

great creative fervor but not a lot of verbal rationalization and very little interchange with other local

firms. All effort focused on the architectural projects at hand.[6]

Nationally, Lundy won a 1961 *Progressive Architecture* honor design award
for his Fairfield County (Connecticut) Unitarian Church (figure 7.14). Another winged structure thrusting to the sky, the church was built from
drawings produced in Sarasota. A second Unitarian Church in Hartford,

7.14 **First Unitarian Church of Fairfield County,** Westport, Connecticut, 1961–1962; Victor Lundy, architect

7.15 | **First Unitarian Church,** Hartford, Connecticut, 1962–1963 (ceiling under construction); Victor Lundy, architect

Connecticut, in the shape of a circle (figure 7.15) was also done in Lundy's Sarasota office. Boyd Blackner ably ran Lundy's office there until it finally closed in 1963.[7]

Although the two best-known Sarasota architects of the 1950s—Paul Rudolph and Victor Lundy—were gone, their Florida work was featured in color in a 1962 *Look* magazine article on American architecture and its future.[8] Lundy's featured project, the Herron residence, Venice, was a birdlike wood-roof enclosure that perched on the ground with its round garage tucked under one wing (figure 7.16). Rudolph's was the Deering residence, Casey Key (figure 7.17). Temple-like in appearance, the structure was sited on a stretch of remote beach overlooking the Gulf of Mexico. Its three stories of varied interior space levels with views to the water was supported by load-bearing exposed block walls spanned by with flexicore precast concrete roof units.

7.16   **Herron residence,** Venice, Florida, 1958–1959; Victor Lundy, architect

7.17   **Deering residence,** Casey Key, 1959–1960; Paul Rudolph, architect

Philip Hiss, no longer a Sarasota County School Board member, now devoted his local time to residential development, writing, and a new interest: establishment of a four-year college in Sarasota. Seeing an opportunity to further higher education in Sarasota, Hiss successfully appealed to the Ford Foundation in 1961 for a $100,000 grant to study the possibility of establishing a liberal arts college there. The initial public response was positive and soon a board of trustees was established.[9]

In Sarasota the third-generation architects were making themselves known. Frank Folsom Smith, who had worked in Victor Lundy's and the Zimmermans' offices, began his practice with the largest commission ever awarded a local: the Plymouth Harbor high-rise adult living facility on St. Armands Key (figure 7.18). Taking over four years to plan and build, its finished twenty-eight-story tower was appropriately isolated on a narrow stretch of land edged by the bay. Each three floors of perimeter residential

7.18   **Plymouth Harbor adult living high-rise facility,**

St. Armands Key, 1962–1966;

Frank Folsom Smith and Louis Schneider, associated architects

7.19   **Plymouth Harbor adult living high-rise facility,**

St. Armands Key, 1962–1966

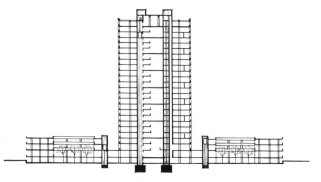

Plate 1   **McDonald residence,** Siesta Key, 1965; Tim Seibert, architect

Plate 2 | **Plymouth Harbor adult living high-rise facility,** St. Armands Key, 1962–1966; Frank Folsom Smith and Louis Schneider, associated architects

Plate 3   **Weld beach house,** Boca Grande, 1966; Carl Abbott, architect

Plate 4   **Brosmith office-residence,** Pound Ridge, New York, 1966; Bert Brosmith, architect

Plate 5 | **Strang residence,** Winter Haven, 1966; Gene Leedy, architect

7.20 | **Sarasota Juvenile Detention Facility,** 1963; Bert Brosmith and Frank Folsom Smith, associated architects

units cluster around a common central social space. The concrete structure, clad with architectural concrete perimeter balconies, became the first Sarasota school project to pierce the skyline and gain visual recognition from a considerable distance. Louis Schneider was Smith's associate on the project. The lower-level concrete mushroom canopies that covered parked cars are reminiscent of Lundy's earlier Warm Mineral Springs Inn roof units (figure 7.19).

Frank Smith and Bert Brosmith associated to do the Sarasota Juvenile Detention Facility (figure 7.20). It was a solid masonry-and-concrete structure pierced with slots and openings and screened by lower masonry walls reminiscent of Louis Kahn's work. Its verticality against the strong horizontality of its site gave it a sense of balance.

William Rupp, Bert Brosmith's contemporary in Rudolph's 1950s office, had earlier started his own Sarasota firm with Joseph Farrell, associate. Their

concrete-and-masonry design for Caladesi National Bank in Dunedin also won a *Progressive Architecture* award in 1961 (figure 7.21).

Smaller residential designs continued to make their mark in Sarasota. The Uhr studio-residence (figure 7.22) by Joseph Farrell and William Rupp was completed for the artist and his wife. **A**-frame in outline, it was a dynamic combination of stepped concrete block, sloped cypress boards, glass, and plastic panels, open to its ridge on the inside with high balcony studios above second-level living and first-level bedrooms.

Carl Abbott, the youngest of the third-generation group, received his final architectural degree at Yale while Rudolph was chair there. Reared on Florida's west coast in Ft. Myers, Abbott was very aware of Sarasota architec-

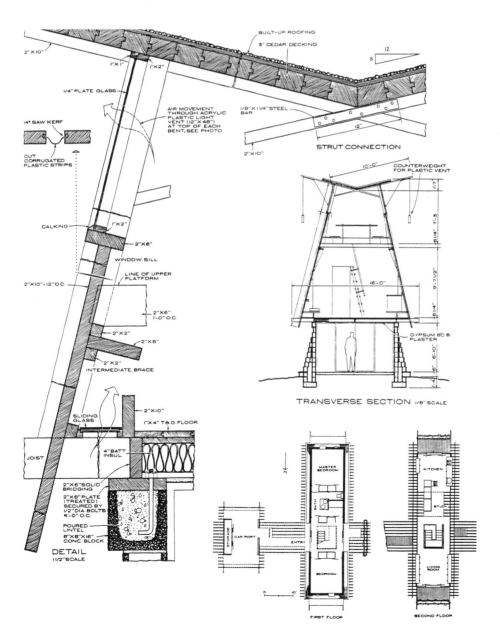

ture. Stays in Norman Foster and Richard Rogers's Team Four London office, Bert Brosmith's studio and I. M. Pei's New York office prepared him for his Sarasota beginning. From Sarasota he designed and completed his first project, the Weld beach house, Boca Grande, Florida, in 1966 (figure 7.23).

Long and low with flat roofs, it resembled a sleek yacht on sand. Its walls were weathered gray cedar siding with bands of glass windows and panels of sliding glass doors. Entry was from a raised wood deck. It was later featured in the 1972 *Architectural Record* Homes Issue.[10]

This complex of main house and guest cottage sits as an angled **L** to protect a landward tropical garden from Gulf of Mexico winds and weather. Made up of a system of angles and triangles, the house interior space becomes layers of inner penetrating horizontal bands separated from the main ceiling by glass. The void in one plane is sometimes the solid in another. Living, dining, and bedroom walls are angled in Abbott's design to take advantage of views and breezes. The main level is a raised platform with exterior angled and curved wood decks surrounding the living areas. All structures on the landward side are tied together with enclosing stuccoed walls. "Fractured geometric forms" describes the Weld beach house. His constant search to combine segmented parts to produce a whole identifies Carl Abbott as author of this design.

Still tied to Sarasota was Gene Leedy, who from Winter Haven was concurrently investigating the idea of more solidarity in his designs. He replaced his original perimeter wood screen walls in his own 1956 home with exposed concrete-block walls to match the main house walls. Intrigued with the idea of using precast, prestressed concrete Ts, Leedy applied the technique to the small two-story office he designed and built for himself in 1961 (figure 7.24). Of sandblasted concrete double Ts, carefully crafted and site-assembled to rest on precast concrete beams and columns, the office structure is enclosed by walls of tall sliding glass panels on three sides. Beyond are exposed Ocala-block courtyard privacy walls totally encompassing the office studio. These walls are finished with a cap course of red brick. By proportioning the Ts with deeper stems and manipulating the roof edges

7.24 **Gene Leedy architectural office,** Winter Haven, Florida, 1961; Gene Leedy, architect

along the perimeter, Leedy established his signature concrete double **T** design, which has continued to appear in his projects throughout his career. Leedy was also instrumental in designing monumental aluminum-frame sliding glass doors that were the first manufactured by a Florida company.

Tim Seibert also explored the possibilities of the double **T** concrete units in the construction of a county beach facility on Siesta Key (figure 7.25). Of concrete block walls with the columns and beams cast on site, the structure's higher precast **T** roof units shade showers, lockers, and toilets below.

7.25   **Sarasota County beach facility,** Siesta Key, 1962; Tim Seibert, architect

What is unique here is the splayed design of the columns and beams coupled with the staggered edges of the **T** roof. Outdoor showers, pump room, and storage space are located in the lower adjacent buildings. At night the front portion becomes a pavilion for social events.

Thus, beginning with the design of the 1958–1959 Sarasota High School of layered concrete sunscreen panels, the Sarasota work of Rudolph's successors also began to move toward more permanent forms in their architectural constructions, while keeping the lightness of feeling achieved in the 1950s through the release of space between their interpenetrating forms.

In contrast, Ralph Twitchell and his oldest son, Tolyn, practicing together since 1959, continued to design lighter steel- and wood-framed residences such as the Hutchinson residence on Casey Key (figure 7.26). A one-story flat-roofed structure at the water's edge, it is a combination enclosure of glassed and screened spaces that interplay.

7.26   **Hutchinson residence,** Casey Key, 1962; Ralph Twitchell and Tolyn Twitchell, architects

7.27   **Carlisle "Circus" residence,** Big Pass, Siesta Key, 1964; Ralph Twitchell and Tolyn Twitchell, architects

A second, more unusual residential structure done by the two was the Carlisle residence, Big Pass (figure 7.27). Of two circular elements—the main house and a guest cottage—with conical metal roofs, it recalls circus tents with a tensile steel quality. Inside, its two-story living space is divided with steel stairs and bedroom balcony units.

By this time—1962—a number of changes were occurring in Sarasota's political, economic, and community agendas. Among them, Hiss's proposed liberal arts college was gaining support and had a name: New College. A board of trustees and a president had been selected and created a search committee to choose an architect to do a master plan and initial building design. Much excitement was generated because of the magnitude of the project and the local availability of talented architects.

An undercurrent of distrust for Sarasota architects, however, was being generated by the local newspaper, certain politicians, and some community leaders, who directed the search toward nationally known architects outside of Sarasota. Hiss no longer had control, and the Board's final decision was to hire I. M. Pei of New York as the architect for the college master plan and buildings. Bert Brosmith was picked to be Pei's local representative and work began on the master plan (figure 7.28). So much antagonism had been generated during the selection process that opposition mounted against the college itself, in the face of which the trustees were financially forced to take a compromise college site that was bisected by Highway 41.

7.28   **New College dormitory buildings,** Sarasota, 1964–1965;

I. M. Pei, New York, architect, Bert Brosmith, associated architect

But the strength of the Sarasota architects' work continued to stand above the confusion of community attitudes toward New College. Bert Brosmith was selected by *Architectural Forum* as one of 14 United States architects in "New Talent for the Sixties." His Sarasota Junior High School design was featured in the article. Mark Hampton's concrete-and-brick Tampa residence (figure 7.29) was named the National 1963 Horizon House winner. Jack West's 1964 Courtyard house, Bird Key, Sarasota (figure 7.30), received the national "Homes for Better Living" award.

Despite the community feeling toward local architects, Jack West was selected to do the new Sarasota City Hall in 1965. Located downtown on First Street on a generous double city block, the City Hall was to be built of brick, concrete, and copper "to last a thousand years," according to West. A contemporary clock tower was included in the design.

When the low construction bid came in 40 percent above the estimated cost, West was forced to completely revise his plans and specifications. Fortunately the low bidder was a sympathetic local contractor who had worked with West before; the two together were able to bring the construction cost within budget, and City Hall was built in 1966 (figure 7.31).

Retained from the original concept were the elevated, platformed entrance podium with its sculpture, reflecting pools, walks and walled parking areas. Gone were the distinctive clock tower, brickwork, and copper. The changes in building proportions and exterior finish materials gave the final City Hall a spare, almost stripped look, without the detail and clock tower to enrich and identify its public function.

In 1965 the acknowledged "father" of the Sarasota school, Ralph Twitchell, retired at age 75, leaving his example of practice for the younger architects to follow.[11] By 1967, the problems with and constraints on architectural design at New College had become so great that I. M. Pei resigned from the project. Bert Brosmith soon left Sarasota for permanent residence in New York. There he designed and built a modular wood frame set on a sloping site. Living areas within this framework are at the top with entry from upper decks. Access to his architectural office is at lower grade, providing separation of uses in one entity (figure 7.32).

In Winter Haven, Gene Leedy continued to successfully scale precast concrete **T** systems to his smaller residential projects. His ability to use extensive cantilevered balconies from the interior spaces within a rigid modular precast concrete frame, made transparent with his large sliding glass panels, is well shown in his Dorman residence, Winter Haven (figure 7.33). Overlooking a lake, the house was planned as a rectangle with a two-story

7.29   **Horizon House,** Tampa, Florida, 1963; Mark Hampton, architect

7.30   **Coutyard House,** Sarasota, 1964; Jack West, architect

7.32   **Brosmith office-residence,** Pound Ridge, New York, 1966; Bert Brosmith, architect

entry port cochere linked to the main house by a brick-walled courtyard on the front and slim two-story roofs leading to the entrances. Visually protected from the street by a grove of oak trees, one passes the courtyard and enters the living area to the spatial surprise of glass-walled views to the lake on the opposite side of its two-story space. Solidity is provided with brick floors, a brick fireplace and the deep dimensions of the exposed ceiling T-beams. Their linearity visually directs one to the lake view and the balconies. Connected by two sets of open oak-tread stairs, the two-story house becomes three levels on the lakeside with the slope of the land.

Similar in structural concept is Leedy's First National Bank of Cape Canaveral (figure 7.34). Square in plan, two stories high with the capability to expand to three stories, the bank rests on a raised brick podium facing a busy highway. The use of dual columns embracing two sets of open sculptural stairs catches the passing driver's eye both day and night. In the cen-

7.33 **Dorman residence,** Winter Haven, 1963; Gene Leedy, architect

ter between the stair structures is a two-story-high banking lobby and its adjacent one-story teller and office spaces. The exposed concrete **T**-beams continue inside as structure and as rhythmic ceiling decoration.

Leedy's largest **T**-beam project was the unbuilt seven-story Florida Tile Company building planned for Lakeland (figure 7.35). Square in plan, the structure's main columns, beams and **T**-beams were all to be precast, with the finished units erected on-site. The central elevator, stair, and toilet walls that stiffen the total structure were to be installed after each floor frame was erected. Continuous outside balconies were formed with double pre-cast panels that made perimeter planter-box rails.

Perhaps his best domestic design is the Strang residence, in Winter Haven (figure 7.36). A subtle combination of double **T**s, precast beams, and wood trussed gabled roofs resting on the uppermost beams, this large 4,000-

7.34   **First National Bank,** Cape Canaveral, Florida, 1963; Gene Leedy, architect

7.35   **Florida Tile Company Building,** Lakeland, Florida, 1960 (unbuilt); Gene Leedy, architect

square-foot dwelling surrounds a pleasant tree-filled court on four sides (figure 7.37). Again, cantilevered balconies on two levels focus to outside views of lake, land, and trees as well as inward to the courtyard. The details of exposed concrete, concrete block, brick trim, planters, and clay tile roofs complete this unusual composition (figure 7.38).

The concrete **T** structural system enabled Leedy economically to form larger, bold spaces at relatively low square footage costs. However, as an exposed low-cost shell, the factory finish lacked the delicacy and finesse of his earlier non-concrete work. In this situation, he developed several levels of finish and cost to suit the client's pocketbook. The range went from basic, exposed, rough factory finishes to sandblasted architectural concrete with brick, marble, and wood-paneled surfaces. So imaginative were his concrete designs that numerous types of buildings—offices, doctors' clinics, clubs, banks, schools, and residences—have been constructed throughout Florida with this system.[12]

In Sarasota, however, the quality of architectural projects began to decline. The demands of owners, many of whom were now large out-of-town development companies, were more important than the design opportunities their projects offered architects. *Architectural Forum,* an accurate barometer of this period, in June 1967 reprinted part of the keynote speech made a decade earlier by the late Henry Luce at the 1957 American Institute of Architects convention.[13] Luce noted at that time that the American revolution in architecture was in place, poised to take on the most "staggering mass of building ever done on this planet." He made the case that "for 200 years the American people [had] been faithful to one dominant purpose—namely, to the establishment of a form of government [Democracy]. Secondly, that purpose [had] been now fulfilled and we [were] seized by a broader challenge, namely the shaping of a civilization. . . . This creative response to challenge will be most vividly expressed in and by architecture."

Henry Luce was in a strong position to make his argument. From his office as editor-in-chief of *Architectural Forum, Time, Life,* and *Fortune* he had seen the rapid, energetic growth of our post–World War II economy, and the rise of American architecture in the world, with the technological means to do what he predicted. Luce cautioned in 1957 that there were two things to be reckoned with: "the appalling amount of ugliness in the American scene . . . and the degradation of democratic taste."

By 1967 the results were as Henry Luce predicted: A high level of building construction had occurred in this country but unfortunately at a low level of architectural competency. Luce, had he lived, would have been disappointed at the failure of the American people, big business, government, and architects to seize the cultural opportunities he envisioned for them in 1957.

In the same 1967 issue of *Architectural Forum* Philip Hiss's article "Whatever Happened to Sarasota?" appeared. Hiss coined the name "The Sarasota School of Architecture" and credited Ralph Twitchell as the "Father" of the movement. The accompanying photographs in the article showed the high-quality work of the "Sarasota School" architects compared to the ordinary construction that had succeeded them (figure 7.39). Hiss concluded: "Sarasota has almost completely surrendered to the big developers and to the East Coast (of Florida) money. There are a number of multi-million dollar projects under way—all them concerned with profits, none of them with architecture."

This developer-driven architecture soon came to dominate the American architectural scene. Theorists like Robert Venturi, rather than attacking this

7.36   **Strang residence,** Winter Haven, 1966; Gene Leedy, architect

7.37   **Strang residence,** section through courtyard

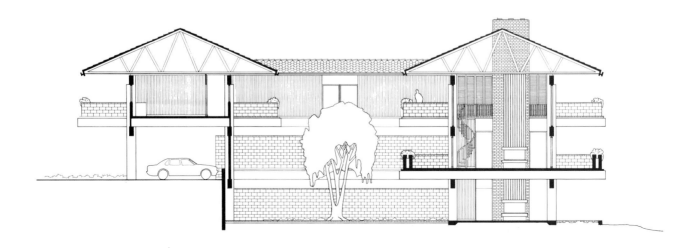

situation, embraced it. The postmodernists, as Venturi and others called themselves, vigorously questioned the essence of work produced in the 1950s and early 1960s. Their new vernacular veneer approach was an immediate success with promoters and developers who needed inexpensive "novelty" coverings to sell their bulk building products. Architects now were required only to design the container, seldom its contents. Architectural fees could be reduced, to the pleasure of developers. The intellectual and philosophical revolt against modern American architecture was complete by the late 1960s.

7.38 | **Strang residence,** detail

7.39 | **Examples of 1960s buildings by Sarasota developers;** no architects

CHAPTER EIGHT

BEYOND SARASOTA

■ Is architecture dead? Some believe that architecture is no longer sustainable as an art form in our present society. "Suspended" might better describe architecture's state in the face of the constant, uncoordinated growth our American built environment has experienced over the last five decades.[1] Many individual Sarasota school projects are now virtually hidden by subsequent development. The town center—Five Points and lower Main Street—has lost its identity with Sarasota Bay, as has the physical downtown. Gone is the relationship between land and water. Missing is the leisure essence that downtown Sarasota had for decades. Lost are the Main Street pier and adjacent boat docks, which gave character to its central waterfront (figure 8.1). There is no longer a sense of place in built Sarasota.

No focus now exists in Sarasota or the United States to create a consistent work environment in which to produce worthy architecture. The weights of relentless production and consumption, coupled with excessive government bureaucracy, unfairly regulate our lives today in America. Architecture must somehow be separated from the oppressive market-government values of the 1990s.

It is ironic that other countries trying to emulate the successes of the United States may have better governmental, economic, and social situations to accomplish what Henry Luce proposed for great American architecture in 1957. Certainly architectural stars, such as Paul Rudolph, have done their best recent work in the Pacific Rim countries. Victor Lundy is also working in Southeast Asia, Mark Hampton in Italy.

Although Sarasota as a center is gone, members of the group have had productive post-Sarasota careers. "Rudolph's initiations and creations have prefigured much of the design that has followed in the United States, Europe, and Japan. He continues to bring new concepts to the world of architecture which find their way into the work of nearly everyone else, becoming part of generalized building practice," according to Mildred Schmertz.[2]

Rudolph best characterizes this creative era (1941 to the present): "moving in space and spatial sequences are the epitome of twentieth-century archi-

8.1   Main Street Pier and Sarasota Bay in 1950

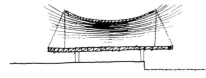

tecture."[3] His diagrams of spatial movement graphically show how he conceived his early projects (figure 8.2). His way of thinking continues in his recent projects. He has designed and built numerous projects in Hong Kong, Singapore, and Jakarta since the mid-1970s. From his New York office he is the designer in association with local Asian architects who produce working drawings and specifications and supervise construction. The potential weak point of this arrangement is lack of communication between the two offices, but the use of facsimile transmissions has diminished this problem in recent years.

One readily sees the connection between Rudolph's early Sarasota ideas and the high-rise buildings that constitute the major part of his work of the last 20 years. His earliest known tower sketch in 1953 (figure 8.3) shows a

8.2	**Spatial movement diagrams by Paul Rudolph**
8.3	**1953 high-rise sketch by Paul Rudolph**
8.4	**Dharmala Sakti building,** Jakarta, 1982–1988;
	Paul Rudolph, design architect, associated with Johannes H. Gunawan, IAI, Jakarta

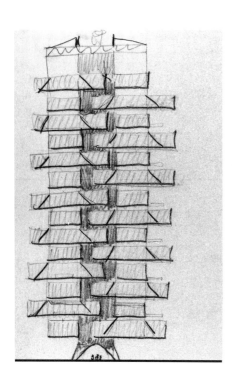

marked similarity to the Dharmala Sakti building, Jakarta (figure 8.4).[4] A very successful regional design, this Asian office tower takes into account the sloped roof form of vernacular Indonesian housing. Paired concrete columns make up its octagonal structural pattern. This geometry creates more views to the outside.

Rudolph's 1950s idea of a central core with office or residential units hung on all four sides by cables from cantilevered beams or trusses at the top persists in his thinking. He visualized mobile home or truck van units plugged into vertical hollow structural tubes carrying the elevators, stairs, and mechanical services for these living units. Practically, the problem was that its rectilinear geometry limits to six or eight floors the weight of hung units per support grid. A more defined drawing of trailer-like modules ap-

8.5 | **1954 tower sketch by Paul Rudolph**

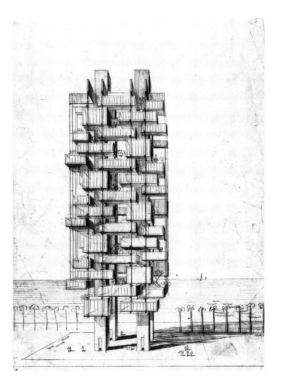

pears in his 1954 Sarasota high-rise sketch of this idea with four service towers (figure 8.5). His Graphic Arts Center project (New York, 1967) shows a series of these units attached to one tall vertical core (figure 8.6). The finished project here is the Colonnade Condominiums, Singapore, 1989 (figure 8.7). Structurally, this building became an economical concrete post-and-beam system that holds the living units with a mass of round support columns at its base. The upper portion is dramatic in appearance, but the whole lacks the vitality of the original tensile idea.

8.6 **Graphic Arts Center,** New York, 1967 (unbuilt); Paul Rudolph, architect

8.8   **Concourse Complex,** Singapore, 1981–1993;

Paul Rudolph, design architect, associated with Architects 61, Singapore

Another Singapore project, the Concourse Complex (1994), was years in the making and is a large-scale mix of office tower, shopping mall, residential hotel, and parking garage (figure 8.8). Its high-energy Rudolphian geometry of serpentine mall and circulation routes culminates in the eight-sided tower with sloped glass windows and distinct diagonal mullions. Its outside appearance is a bit fortress-like and forbidding.

Probably his best Pacific Rim projects are in Hong Kong. The double office and hotel towers of Bond Centre (1989) are again octagons in plan (figure 8.9). The final design generates a distinctive sculptural interlocking of floors on the exterior that is very identifiable at a distance. Bond Centre has become one of three downtown Hong Kong landmarks.

The tallest of Rudolph's Hong Kong skyscraper projects is the 90-story Sino Land Company Office and Hotel Tower Competition entry of 1991 (unbuilt, figure 8.10). Very oriental in feeling and square in plan, its numerous sloped wall sides form strong vertical patterns at its four corners. The pairs of dual corner columns splay in as they rise while decreasing in size. There are six open horizontal mechanical voids in its vertical mass, which give it spatial relief and scale at a distance. The bottom level is open for about 10 stories: if this space were left nearly unencumbered, it should offer the spatial feeling one experiences under the Eiffel Tower that Rudolph alludes to (though the Paris masterpiece presents a more open, lacy structure to the eye than the Hong Kong project).

Bond Centre, Hong Kong, 1984–1988; Paul Rudolph, design architect, associated with Wong & Ouyang (HK) Ltd., Hong Kong

8.10   **Rendering of 90-story Sino Tower: office building, hotel, and commercial facilities, Hong Kong,** 1989 (unbuilt); Paul Rudolph, architect

Paul Rudolph's aesthetic development began with the Florida residential box he separated into structured roof planes and floating platforms subdivided by simple screen walls. The skyscraper to which he gives particular complex geometries and aggressive angularities—described by some as compositional rigorism and even brutalism—remains his current direction. Sometimes dangerous or threatening and always confrontational, his work is not timid architecture. Danger is one of the attractions of his work. "Strong, logical, and independent" describes his character from Florida to today.

Victor Lundy's vigorous, original, flamboyantly shaped spaces on the Florida landscape form an economical means to enclose living, worship, and working architecture. His direction has slowly taken a new turn. Serene, quiet, and appropriate to their surroundings, his more recent buildings show a new strength and maturity. After Sarasota, Lundy's projects became more substantial, such as the IBM Complex in New Jersey (figure 8.11), whose intricate brick patterns and concrete umbrella columns showed a sensitive durability. His model for the Interrama Pyramid of the

8.11 **IBM Complex,** Cranford, New Jersey, 1962; Victor Lundy, architect

8.12   **Interrama Pyramid of the Sun Exhibition Hall,** Miami, Florida, 1965 (unbuilt); Victor Lundy, architect

Sun exhibition hall in Miami showed a mature concept of spatial structure (figure 8.12). His wood shade shelters at the Smithsonian in Washington (figure 8.13), the exquisite wood enclosures at the I. Miller shoe shop in Manhattan (figure 8.14), and his several air structure designs (figure 8.15) displayed a new richness and growth beyond his Sarasota work.

The change to a restrained strength in his work occurred most dramatically with the United States Tax Court Building in Washington, D.C., completed in 1976 with Lyles, Bissett, Carlisle and Wolff Associates (figure 8.16). The building is a rectangular block pulled apart to make four distinct units: office blocks at each end and center rear; the courtroom block cantilevered over the monumental front entry steps, and the fourth podium block concealing two floors of lowest service space. The voids created between blocks are spanned with deeply recessed glass windows that provide light and orientation to the interior. Its scale and quiet dignity, surrounded by nervous concrete government buildings from the 1960s and 1970s, stabilize the neighborhood.

Patience and tenacity were required for Lundy's work on the United States Embassy in Sri Lanka (Ceylon), which took 23 years to complete. Originally designed in 1961 as a circular building with a center courtyard, the project lay dormant until the early 1980s. With a revised program and new require-

8.13 **Smithsonian Sunshade Shelters,** Washington, D.C., 1967; Victor Lundy, architect

8.14   **I. Miller Shoe Salon,** New York, 1965; Victor Lundy, architect

8.15   **Air Structure Pavillions,** 1964–1965, New York World's Fair; Victor Lundy, architect

8.16 **U.S. Tax Court Building and Plaza,** Washington, D.C., 1967–1976;

Victor Lundy, design architect, in association with Lyles, Bisset,

Carlisle & Wolff Associates

ments, the design became a straightforward rectangular double-loaded plan and pattern of concrete vertical openings filled in with a similar pattern of teak security grilles. The hipped tile roof is a sculptural outgrowth of its lower grid (figure 8.17).

Working as the design principal in a large Dallas architectural firm since the mid-1980s, Lundy has been able to do a variety of projects.[5] His largest to date in the United States was the GTE Telephone Operations World Headquarters facility at Irving, Texas, in 1991 (figure 8.18). Its immense size—1.3 million square feet—required first destroying the 82-acre site to accommodate the extensive underground parking and service spaces, then restoring its mesquite-covered hill to complete the construction. Two pinwheel office buildings each step up the hillside, with lakes and a waterfall between the buildings. By placing nearly half of the building bulk underground, Lundy retained human scale. His color palette is effectively keyed to the Texas red sandstone and green landscape of the site.

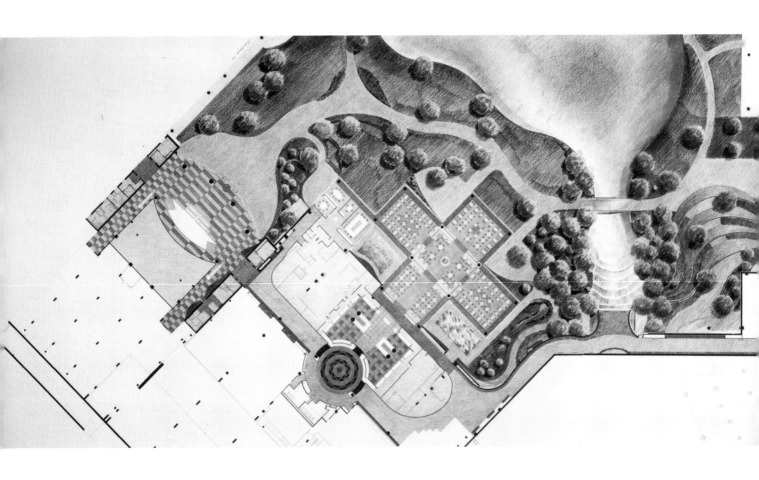

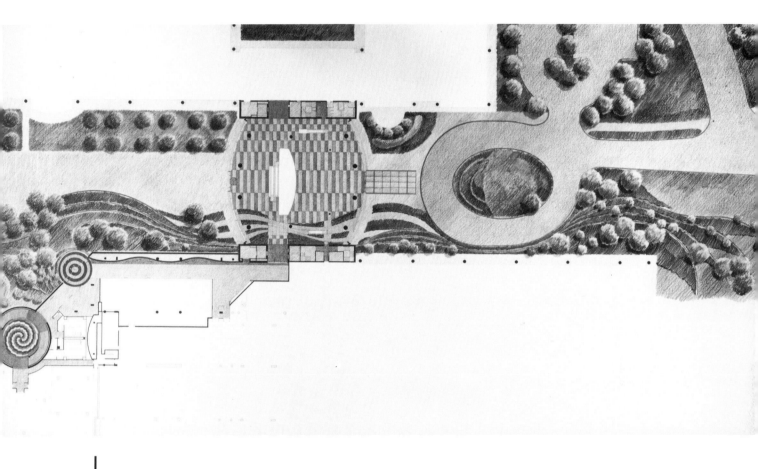

8.18   GTE Operations World Headquarters, Irving, Texas, 1987–1991; Victor Lundy, design principal, with HKS Inc., Dallas

8.19   **Barnett Bank,** Jacksonville, Florida, 1988 (unbuilt); Victor Lundy, design principal, with HKS Inc., Dallas

Lundy has had high-rise projects in both the United States and Pacific Rim countries. In Jacksonville, Florida, dual towers on the St. John's River (the taller is 50 stories) are proposed for Barnett Bank (figure 8.19). Rectangular in plan and gently curved from one edge to the peak at the other, the towers contain exterior observation elevators in their front service cores.

A mixed-use office-hotel-shopping complex has been designed for a developer in Bangkok, Thailand (figure 8.20). Its sloping tower sides frame the horizontal bands of floors. Its distinctive silhouette will be recognizable from different locations in the urban pattern. Lundy's most interesting vertical idea to date is an 80-story office tower proposal (figure 8.21). The needle-thin structural system uses curved, bundled tubes to carry its slender mass skyward. The peak is announced with a final subtle ending of the four curved forms that develop from its base. His affinity for circular plans and rounded spaces remains in his recent work.

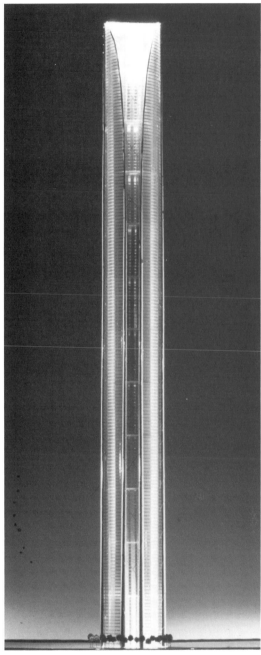

8.20 **Office, hotel, shopping complex,** Bangkok, Thailand, 1992 (unbuilt); Victor Lundy, design principal, with HKS Inc., Dallas

8.21 **Tower proposal,** 1993 (unbuilt); Victor Lundy, design principal, with HKS Inc., Dallas

Always separate from the group, a "lone wolf," as Lundy describes himself, he constantly visualizes his designs in color. Much of the early Sarasota school thinking was in black and white, correlating with the lack of color photography in the early 1950s. Different from the rest of the group, tied to it only chronologically, Lundy continues to grow artistically and architecturally on his own terms.

In the mid-1970s Mark Hampton relocated from Tampa to the more cosmopolitan atmosphere of Miami. From there he has produced an unusual project for Genoa, Italy: a new entrance and below-ground addition to an existing castle that functions as a museum (1991, unbuilt, figure 8.22). The project will add a primary entry at one end of the stone-walled edifice. By following angled ramps and bridges one arrives at the lower main lobby and museum rooms. A small auditorium occupies another level. The minimalist design provides an excellent backdrop for museum pieces shown. The necessary interior furniture, millwork, and accessory items are to be designed by Hampton.

For the 1988 two-story Brabson residence in Tampa (figure 8.23), Hampton relied on the use of water and sculptural openings between the interior and exterior spaces to create spatial interest on an ordinary site. Hampton's strength continues to be total awareness of space, with meticulous detailing of his interiors and exteriors.

In 1990, a Florida architectural design competition was held for the new home of the president of the University of South Florida in Tampa. Gene Leedy and Carl Abbott were two of the five award winners. Leedy's entry (figure 8.24) was chosen to be built. A formal two-story rectangle with courtyards and adjacent outbuildings, it is covered by an umbrella of second-story precast concrete T decks. Its campus gateway design is unmistakably Leedy; its completeness of detail and close relationship to the 1960s design character of the college campus led to its selection by the jury. Now complete, the building's main-floor public spaces are ideal for receptions and entertainment. The two-story living and dining areas flow out into their common exterior courtyard for additional space for large gatherings. Tied together by the common T roofs, the great space allows the visitor to feel the pleasant linear rhythm of these Ts (figure 8.25).

Abbott's entry took a different tack, with a long masonry wall serving as both a gateway to the campus and a buffer from the nearby street traffic (figure 8.26). A second strong entry axis at a 90-degree angle to the first axis provided pedestrian access to and from the campus, culminating in a deck overlooking the tree-covered site. Abbott's building spaces fanned out from the long brick spline responding to different parts of the campus. It was also tied to the campus in its materials, exposed concrete and buff-colored brick.

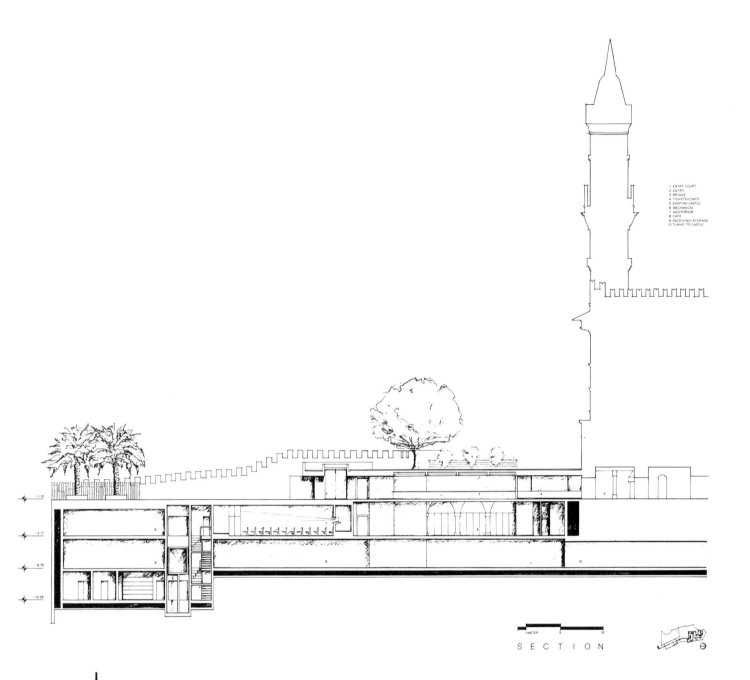

1 ENTRY COURT
2 ENTRY
3 BRIDGE
4 TICKETS/COATS
5 EXISTING CASTLE
6 MECHANICAL
7 AUDITORIUM
8 CAFE
9 RECEIVING/STORAGE
10 TUNNEL TO CASTLE

S E C T I O N

8.22 **Castello Mackenzie-Wolfson,** Genoa, Italy, showing proposed addition by Mark Hampton, 1991 (unbuilt)

8.23 **Brabson residence,** Tampa, 1988; Mark Hampton, architect

8.24   **President's House,** University of South Florida, Tampa, 1994;

Gene Leedy, architect

8.25   **President's House,** University of South Florida, Tampa, 1994

8.26   **President's House entry,** University of South Florida, Tampa, 1990; Carl Abbott, architect

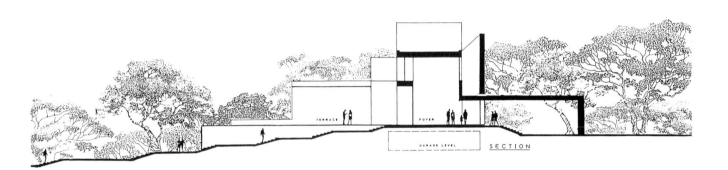

While Leedy's concept was admittedly related to the tradition of columns in southern antebellum architecture, Abbott's design resembles the semicircular concept diagrams of the late Finnish architect Alvar Aalto's work. Abbott's outbuilding added length and scale to the main house wall, with its end-curved wall pulling it also to the campus and main house.

As one can see, the group's results after Sarasota have been mixed. Mixed, also, seems to be the texture of global architecture, perhaps now too diffuse and complex ever again to bear consistent fruit. From 1947, however, there has been an ongoing search by the group for spatial solutions, both interior and exterior, suburban and urban, to satisfy the particular design of each project within its given environment. Most were admittedly achieved on a small scale. Peter Smithson recently observed: "Their [Sarasota] work was not stylistic, but of its culture." [6] Regionalism has always been taken into account: the light, the ambience, the land, the spirit, and the people of the place where the project was located. The group's work was not just a matter of individual designs indiscriminately placed, but an effort to integrate with the surroundings. There has been one twentieth-century constant: explosive urbanization. In the United States we have moved from agrarian living to towns, to cities, and in this century to megacities of 10 million people or more. According to recent growth projections, there will be at least 20 megacities in the world by the year 2000. [7] Several will be new centers hastily thrown together and most will be in third-world countries. This is an incredible opportunity for architects. The question is how to approach the massive problems of urbanism. Can "paradise" be located in megacities?

Rudolph was one of the first to realize this situation.[8] In 1958 he defined urban design as "remodeling, adding, subtracting, reworking, relating, and reforming three-dimensional spaces for human activities including all pedestrian and vehicular systems." His concept of urbanism continues to apply today. To most, modernism seems to have run its course. Well-known architects like Rudolph simply believe architecture is presently taking a detour.

"The idea of the compleat architect—an artist in architecture [and urbanism], concerned to dispose his spaces, to model his masses, to choose and treat his materials, as great architects have always done, in such a way as to achieve compositions, works of art"[9]—must be revived to solve these problems. But can architecture still be an art as well as a technological process for solving the larger problems of shelter? The example of the Sarasota school of architecture stands as one of the best models for such a development.

Central to the 1941–1966 movement are the following beliefs and rules:

1.   Space is the essence of architecture/urbanism.

2.   Architecture must function.

3.   Architecture must be honest, be rooted in reason, and follow a logical vocabulary of building.

4.   Land, water, sky, climate, and atmosphere must be respected.

5.   Use the new technologies.

6.   Make uncommon use of common materials.

7.   There must be constant renewal through continued experimentation and expansion of building vocabularies.

8.   Make a conscious effort to reconcile new architectural/urban ideas with the contemporary social, political, and cultural fabric.

BIOGRAPHIES OF THE ARCHITECTS

■ The outline biographies that follow summarize the careers of these architects, who, to the best of the author's knowledge and research, were active in Sarasota during all or part of the period between 1941 and 1966:

Carl Abbott (b. 1935)

Boyd Blackner (b.1933)

Bert Brosmith (b. 1928)

Joseph Farrell (b. 1932)

Mark Hampton (b. 1923)

Philip Hiss (1910–1988)

Gene Leedy (b. 1928)

Victor Lundy (b. 1923)

Paul Rudolph (b. 1918)

William Rupp (b. 1927)

Tim Seibert (b. 1927)

Frank Folsom Smith (b. 1931)

Ralph S. Twitchell (1890–1978)

Tolyn Twitchell (b. 1928)

Jack West (b. 1922)

These architects were also active during the period, but insufficient information is available about their careers for separate biographies: James Durden, Phil Hall (deceased), Phil Hammill, James Holiday (deceased), Louis Schneider, Col. Roland Sellew (deceased), Carl Volmer, Joan and Ken Warriner, Beth Waters, Don Wilkinson, Ralph Zimmerman (deceased), William Zimmerman (deceased).

James Carl Abbott

1935	Born 1935, Darien, Georgia. Parents James Carl and Jessie Kay Wing Abbott.
1951–1954	Family moved to Ft. Myers, Florida.
1954–1959	Attended University of Florida. Received Bachelor of Architecture degree, *cum laude,* 1959.
1959–1964	U.S. Army Reserve.
1959–1961	Employed by Bert Brosmith, Architect, Sarasota.
1961–1962	Attended Yale University. Received Master of Architecture degree, 1962.
1962–1963	Employed by Architects Hawaii, Ltd., Honolulu, Hawaii.
1963–1964	Employed by Team Four (Norman Foster and Richard Rogers), London, England. Travel and study in Europe. Design instructor at Regent Street Polytechnic Institute, London.
1965	Employed by I. M. Pei, Architect, New York.
1966	Registered architect. Established own practice, Sarasota.
1966	Weld beach house, Punta Gorda, Florida. (*Architectural Record* House, 1972.)
1966	Ringling School Studios, Sarasota.
1977	First Prize, Shelter Competition, St. Petersburg, Florida. U.S. patent awarded 1980.
1979	Deering residence, Siesta Key, Sarasota.
1981	Lido bayfront residence, Sarasota.
1982	Gregg beach house, Siesta Key, Sarasota.
1985	St. Thomas More Church complex, Sarasota.
1986	Fellow, American Institute of Architects.

1986   One-man architectural exhibition at New College/University of South Florida, Sarasota. Awarded AIA Florida/Caribbean Region Medal of Honor for continuing design excellence.

1990   Placed in President's House competition, University of South Florida, Tampa.

1966–   Private practice, Sarasota.
present

Boyd Blackner

1933	Born August 29, 1933, Salt Lake City, Utah. Parents Lester and Anna Blackner.
1951–1956	Attended the University of Utah. Received Bachelor of Architecture degree and Bachelor of Fine Arts.
1955	Married Elizabeth Ann Castleton, Salt Lake City, Utah.
1956	Assistant landscape architect, National Parks Service, Mt. Rainier, Washington.
1957	Job captain with Cannon, Smith and Gustavson, Salt Lake City, Utah.
1958–1959	Employed by Hellmuth, Obata and Kassabaum, St. Louis, Missouri.
1959	Employed by Caudill, Rowlett and Scott, Houston, Texas.
1959–1963	Project architect with Victor A. Lundy, Sarasota, Florida.
1960–1961	First Unitarian Church of Fairfield County, Westport, Connecticut.
1961	U.S. Embassy (first design), Colombo, Sri Lanka.
1962	Sierra Blanca Ski Resort, Lincoln National Forest, Ruidoso, New Mexico.
1963	St. Mark American Lutheran Church, Orlando, Florida.
1963–1964	First Unitarian Congregational Society Church, Hartford, Connecticut.
1960–1963	Received architectural registrations in Florida and Utah.
1978	National American Institute of Architects Honor Award for the Kearns/Daynes/Alley Annex, Salt Lake City, Utah.
1978	Fellow, American Institute of Architects.
1963–present	Private practice in Salt Lake City, Utah.

Bert Brosmith

1928	Born July 1, Hartford, Connecticut. Parents Allan E. and Georgette (Comeau) Brosmith.
1946–1947	U.S. Army Signal Corps photographer, stationed in Japan.
1947–1952	Enrolled in architecture program at University of Pennsylvania. Received Bachelor of Architecture degree (1953).
1953	Attended Harvard University (spring 1953). Awarded Fulbright Scholarship to study in England.
1953–1954	Graduate fellow, Department of Town Planning, University of London. Travel in Europe and British Isles.
1954	Author of "*London—An Urban Framework*" with H. Alan Wightman.
1955	Employed by Paul Rudolph. First Project: "Family of Man" exhibition installed at Museum of Modern Art, New York.
1955–1960	In charge of Florida office of Paul Rudolph.
1955	U.S. Embassy, Amman, Jordan (project).
1957–1958	Riverview High School, Sarasota.
1958–1959	Sarasota Senior High School.
1959	Deering residence, Casey Key.
1960	Established own firm in Sarasota, Florida.
1961	Sarasota Junior High School addition. Dental office building for James Paulk, D.D.S., Sarasota.
1961	Married Cathrina Boman, Sarasota.

1961	Selected by *Architectural Forum* as one of 14 architects in *Forum* issue devoted to "New Talent for the Sixties."
1962	Addition to Philip H. Hiss residence, Lido Shores, Sarasota.
1963	Juvenile Detention Facility for Sarasota County (with Frank Folsom Smith).
1964	Dorothea Dawson residence, Sarasota.
1964–1965	Associated architect with I. M. Pei, New York, for East Campus, New College, Sarasota.
1964	Appointed visiting design critic, Yale University Department of Architecture.
1965–1969	Architect with Perkins and Will, White Plains, New York.
1969–1975	With Juster, Brosmith, Levine, Architects and Planners, New York City.
1976–present	Private practice in Pound Ridge, New York.

Joseph Farrell

1932	Born 1932 Gastonia, North Carolina. Parents Ralph and Norma Farrell.
1947	Family moved to Sarasota, Florida.
1950–1954	Enrolled for three and one-half years in architecture program at University of Florida.
1950–1954	Worked part-time for Paul Rudolph, Sarasota, Florida.
1955–1957	U.S. Army, tour of duty in Europe.
1957–1959	Completed one and one-half years of architecture program at University of Florida. Received Bachelor of Architecture degree, January 1959.
1959	Designer with Carl Volmer, Architect, Sarasota, Florida.
1959–1961	Associated with William Rupp, Architect, Sarasota, Florida.
1960	Farrell Commercial Building (with William Rupp). Caladesi National Bank, Dunedin, Florida (with William Rupp). Received *Progressive Architecture* Design Award, 1961.
1961	Uhr residence-studio (with William Rupp), Sarasota, Florida. Received New York Chapter AIA, First Award Citation, 1964. Scott Office Building (with William Rupp), Sarasota, Florida.
1961	Received architectural registrations in Florida and Hawaii.
1961–1975	Employed as designer and then associate in office of Lemmon, Freeth, Haines and Jones, Honolulu, Hawaii.
1975– present	Design principal in office of Hawaii, Ltd. (formerly Lemmon, Freeth, Haines and Jones), Honolulu, Hawaii.

Mark Garrison Hampton

1923	Born July 17, Tampa, Florida. Parents Ham and Laura Hampton.
1941	Enrolled at Georgia Institute of Technology in Beaux-Arts architecture program.
1943–1946	U.S. Army, infantry company commander, 42nd Division, Third Army, in Europe.
1946–1949	Returned to Georgia Tech; received his B.S. degree (1948) and Bachelor of Architecture degree (1949).
1949	Summer: School of Architecture, Fontainebleau, France. Toured Europe.
1950	Taught at Georgia Tech School of Architecture. Employed part-time at Bodin and Lamberson, Atlanta.
1951	Employed by Twitchell and Rudolph, Sarasota.
1952	Received architectural registration in Florida. Established own firm in Tampa, Florida.
1953	Residence-clinic for Dr. George W. Morrison, Tampa. Laura Hampton residence, Tampa.
1956	Jordan residence, Lake Wales, Florida. Received 1957 Homes for Better Living Award sponsored by *Time, House and Home,* and the American Institute of Architects.
1958	Galloway's Furniture Showroom, Tampa.
1960	St. Mary's Episcopal Church, Tampa. Weiss residence, Savannah, Georgia.
1961	Amaryllis Park Primary School, Sarasota.
1962	McIntosh Student Center Middle School, Sarasota.

1963	Horizon House, Tampa. Received First Place, 1963 National Horizon Homes Program.
1966–1973	Associated with H. Herbert Johnson Associates, Miami and Tampa.
1967	Webb residence, Tampa.
1967	Fellow, American Institute of Architects.
1965–1989	Director, Patrick Lannan Museum Foundation, Palm Beach, Florida.
1987	Wolfe residence, Miami.
1987	Received AIA Florida/Caribbean Region Honor Award for design accomplishments.
1987– present	Micky Wolfson, "Wolfsonian" Museum, Miami Beach and Genoa, Italy.
1974– present	Private practice in Coconut Grove, Florida.

Philip Hanson Hiss

1910	Born February 2, Brooklyn, New York. Parents Philip Hanson and Caroline (Dow) Hiss.
1916–1928	Attended various private schools.
1930–1931	Toured South America on a Harley-Davidson motorcycle.
1932	Took inaugural Pan-American Clipper flight from Rio de Janeiro to Miami.
mid-1930s	Worked for Hess, New York photographer.
late 1930s	Sailed around the world.
1939	Lived on the island of Bali for one year. Author of the book *Bali*.
1940–1941	Moved to New Canaan, Connecticut, and became a residential developer.
1942–1946	Served during World War II in OSS., Far Eastern Division.
1946–1947	Served as assistant diplomat in charge of education in Holland.
1948	Took sailboat trip around east coast of United States. Picked Sarasota as a place to settle.
1949	Married Shirley de Camp Holt, Sarasota.
1949–1950	Developer of first four houses on Lido Key. Ralph and William Zimmerman were his first architects.
1951	Builder of first two-story concrete house on Sarasota Bay.
1952	Elected to Sarasota County School Board; subsequently elected chairman.
1954	Hiss "Umbrella" Residence, Lido Shores, designed by Paul Rudolph.
1956–1962	Hiss awards Sarasota County School projects to local designer-architects.

1958	New College, Sarasota, conceived. Hiss received Ford Foundation Grant to establish college.
1965	Writer for *Tampa Tribune*. Family moved to London, England.
1967	Author of *Architectural Forum* magazine article "Whatever Happened to Sarasota?"
1988	Died, London, England.

Gene Leedy

1928	Born February 6, Isaban, West Virginia. Parents Cecil H. and Ethyl F. Leedy.
1943–1947	Enrolled at University of Florida. Received Associate of Arts degree.
1947–1950	Continued architecture program at University of Florida. Received Bachelor of Architecture degree.
1948	Honorable Mention, Hidden Talent Competition, Museum of Modern Art, New York.
1950	Married Katherine Hoge, Arlington, Virginia. Employed by Robert Murphey, Architect, Orlando.
1950–1951	Employed by Ralph and William Zimmerman, Sarasota. Designed several Sarasota residences on his own during this time.
1951	Employed by Paul Rudolph, Sarasota.
1952	Received architectural registration in Florida.
1952–1954	U.S. Air Force, New York City.
1953	Work exhibited at International Architecture Exhibit, São Paulo, Brazil.
1954	Established own firm, Sarasota.
1955	Moved office to Winter Haven, Florida.
1956	Prototype house for Craney Homes, Inc., Winter Haven.
1958	Brentwood Elementary School, Sarasota (associated with William Rupp).
1959	Lake Region Yacht and Country Club, Winter Haven, in collaboration with Paul Rudolph.
1960	Florida Tile Industries Building (project), Lakeland, Florida. Winter Haven City Hall.

1960	Married Marjorie Ingram King, Tampa.
1961	Leedy Architectural Office, Winter Haven.
1963	Dorman residence, Winter Haven. SAE Fraternity House, Gainesville. First National Bank of Cape Canaveral, Florida.
1965	Prototype houses for Levitt & Sons, Rockledge, Florida.
1966	Work exhibited at Tampa Bay Art Center.
1969	"The Architectural Photography of Gene Leedy" exhibit, Ridge Art Association, Winter Haven.
1988	Received AIA Florida/Caribbean Region Medal of Honor for design accomplishments.
1990	First Place, President's House Competition, University of South Florida, Tampa.
1992	Fellow, American Institute of Architects.
1955– present	Private practice, Winter Haven, Florida.

Victor Alfred Lundy

1923	Born February 1, Manhattan. Parents Alfred Henry and Rachel Lundy.
1939–1943	Enrolled at New York University. Later in Beaux-Arts architecture program.
1943–1946	U.S. Army, infantry sergeant, Third Army, in Europe. Wounded in action, awarded Purple Heart.
1946–1947	Enrolled in Architecture program at Harvard University. Received Bachelor of Architecture degree, 1947.
1947	Married Shirley Corwin, New York City.
1948	Continued master's program at Harvard with Walter Gropius; received Master of Architecture degree.
1948–1950	Awarded Rotch Traveling Scholarship by Boston Society of Architects. Traveled in Europe, Middle East, and North Africa.
1950–1951	Employed with various architectural firms in New York City.
1951	Received architectural registrations in New York and California.
1951	Ben Stahl residence, Sarasota.
1954	Established own firm in Sarasota, Florida.
1954	Drive-in Garden Sanctuary, Nokomis Presbyterian Church, Venice, Florida, received national attention.
1956	Sarasota Chamber of Commerce Building, published extensively. Architectural design consultant, Inter-American Center, Miami. Bee Ridge Presbyterian Church, Sarasota.
1957	Display of work in "America Builds" exhibition in Berlin International Architectural Exposition. Tourist Center, Silver Springs, Florida, displayed at São Paulo, Brazil, International Biennial Exhibition.

1958	Work Exhibited at 5th Congress, Union Internationale des
	Architectes, Moscow. Alta Vista Elementary School, new
	addition, Sarasota.
1958–1966	Visiting lecturer at Columbia Unversity, Yale University, Uni-
	versity of Arkansas, and University of California, Berkeley.
1958–1970	St. Paul's Lutheran Church projects, Sarasota. Numerous
	other churches designed and built in Florida.
1959	Herron residence, Venice, Florida, received First Honor
	Award, AIA, in cooperation with *House and Home* and
	McCall's magazines. Galloway's Furniture Showroom,
	Sarasota.
1960	Established office in New York City. Married Anstis Man-
	ton Burwell, New York City.
1960–1961	First Unitarian Church of Fairfield County, Westport, Con-
	necticut. Received 1960 *Progressive Architecture* Unbuilt
	Design Award.
1961–1984	Awarded U.S. Embassy, Colombo, Sri Lanka. Completed
	1984. Accorded 1988 U.S. Presidential Award for its design
	from NEA.
1965	USAI Exhibit, "Architecture—USA", U.S. Department of
	State, for exhibition abroad.
1965–1967	Traveling Exhibition Building and Exhibit, U.S. Atomic En-
	ergy Commission.
1967	Fellow, American Institute of Architects.
1967	Smithsonian Institution shade and recreation shelters,
	Washington, D.C.

1975	Visiting professor and lecturer, School of Architecture, California Polytechnic State University, San Luis Obispo, and University of New Mexico, Albuquerque.
1976	Expo '70 Exhibition, Osaka, Japan.
1976–1984	Established Victor A. Lundy & Associates, Houston.
1976–1984	Adjunct professor of architecture, College of Architecture, University of Houston.
1984–present	Design principal and vice-president, H.K.S., Inc., Dallas.

Paul Marvin Rudolph

1918	Born October 23, Elkton, Kentucky. Parents Reverend Keener L. and Eurye (Stone) Rudolph.
1935–1940	Enrolled at Alabama Polytechnic Institute in Beaux-Arts architecture program. Received Bachelor of Architecture degree.
1940–1941	Employed by E. B. Van Koeren, Birmingham, Alabama.
1941	Five months' employment with Ralph Twitchell, Sarasota.
1941	Entered Harvard Graduate School of Design.
1942	Joined U.S. Naval Reserve. Attended officers' training schools at MIT and Princeton.
1943–1946	Stationed at Brooklyn Naval Yard.
1946	Returned to both Twitchell's office and Harvard.
1947	Received his Master of Architecture degree from Harvard. Finney house and guest cottage project (with Twitchell office), published extensively.
1947	Miller guest cottage and residence, Casey Key, Sarasota.
1948	Awarded Wheelright Traveling Fellowship in Architecture. Traveled in Europe 1948 and 1949.
1948	Revere Quality House, Siesta Key, Sarasota. Rudolph became Twitchell's associate.
1948–1950	Healy ("Cocoon") guest house, Siesta Key, Sarasota.
1950	Editor, special edition of *L'Architecture d'aujourd'hui* entitled "The Spread of an Idea." Received architectural registration in New York. Made Twitchell's partner.

1951–1952	Designer of Good Design Exhibition at Merchandise Mart, Chicago, and Museum of Modern Art, New York.
1951	Twitchell-Rudolph partnership dissolved in March. Both Twitchell and Rudolph formed their own Sarasota offices.
1952	Walker residence, Sanibel Island.
1952	Knott residence 1 (project), Yankeetown.
1953	Hiss residence (Umbrella House), Siesta Key, Sarasota.
1954	Cohen residence 1 (project), Siesta Key, Sarasota. Won best of 1955 *Progressive Architecture* Design Competition out of over 500 nationally submitted entries.
1954	Accorded Outstanding Young Architect Award, São Paulo, Brazil, International Competition.
1954–1955	Designed and installed "Family of Man" exhibition at Museum of Modern Art, New York.
1955	Awarded U.S. Embassy, Amman, Jordan (project).
1956	Architectural Design Consultant, Inter-American Center, Miami.
1957	Bradenton-Sarasota Airport 1 (project).
1958	Riverview Junior High School, Sarasota.
1958–1965	Chairman, Department of Architecture, Yale University.
1960	Sarasota Senior High School addition.
1960	Milam residence, Jacksonville.
1965	Exhibit, "Architecture—USA", U.S. Department of State, for exhibition abroad.
1966	Established office in New York City.

1967	Paul Rudolph retrospective exhibition, Tampa Bay Art Center. Traveling show continued to Jacksonville, Gainesville, and Atlanta.
1969	Medal of Honor, American Institute of Architects, New York City.
1970	Fellow, American Institute of Architects.
1976	Fellowship, American Society of Interior Designers.
1989	Gold Medal, Florida/Caribbean Region, American Institute of Architects.
1966–present	Paul Rudolph, Architect, New York City.

William Rupp

1927	Born August 25, Philadelphia, Pennsylvania. Parents Frank J. and Sarah (Hibbs) Rupp.
1945–1946	U.S. Army, Field Artillery.
1946–1949	Employed as laboratory assistant and laborer.
1949–1952	Enrolled at University of Florida in architecture program. Received Bachelor of Architecture degree, 1953
1952	Commissioned in U.S. Army.
1953–1955	Employed at the office of Paul Rudolph, Sarasota.
1954	Received architectural registration in Florida.
1955–1964	Established own firm in Sarasota, Florida.
1956	Married Gwendolyn O'Rourke.
1957	Willis residence, Sarasota.
1958	Hatt residence, Sarasota.
1959	Brentwood Elementary School, Sarasota (associated with Gene Leedy).
1960	Caladesi National Bank, Dunedin, Florida. Received *Progressive Architecture* Design Award (with Joseph Farrell associate).
1961	Uhr studio-residence, Sarasota (with Joseph Farrell).
1965–1966	Moved architectural practice to Naples, Florida.
1965	Rupp residence, Naples.
1968–1972	Designer and associate architect with Morris Ketchum, Jr., and Associates, New York.
1969	Received architectural registration in New York.

1972–1978 Project architect with Callister, Payne and Bischoff, Am-

herst, Massachusetts.

1976 Received architectural registration in Massachusetts. Es-

tablished private practice, Amherst, Massachusetts.

1978– Full-time teaching appointment, Art Department, University

present of Massachusetts.

Edward J. (Tim) Seibert

1927	Born September 27, Seattle, Washington. Parents Edward C. and Elizabeth G. Seibert.
1942	Mother moved family to Sarasota, Florida. Father in U.S. Navy.
1945	Joined U.S. Navy flight program. Honorably discharged, 1946.
1947–1950	Attended Stanford University. Majored in Art.
1950–1952	Enrolled in architecture program at University of Florida. Received Bachelor of Architecture degree, January 1953.
1952	Completed his first house, Seibert residence, Sarasota.
1953–1955	Worked for various Sarasota architectural and construction firms.
1955	Received architectural registration in Florida. Opened his own office.
1955– present	Various speculative residences and work for Arvida Corporation, Sarasota area.
1961	Field Club additions, Sarasota. Godfrey residence, Siesta Key, Sarasota, in *Architectural Record* homes issue.
1962	County Recreation Center, Siesta Key.
1965	John McDonald residence, Sarasota.
1966	Cooney residence, Sarasota.
1975	Wendel Kent guest house, Siesta Key.
1983–1984	Bay Plaza Condominiums, Sarasota.
1955– present	Edward J. Seibert, AIA, Architect and Planner, PA, Sarasota.

Frank Folsom Smith

1931	Born June 21, Philadelphia, Pennsylvania. Parents Frank F. and Ernestine B. Smith.
1932	Family moved to Virginia Beach, Virginia.
1947–1949	Attended Virginia Polytechnic Institute.
1949–1952	Enrolled at University of Virginia. Received Bachelor of Economics degree, 1952.
1954–1957	Enrolled in School of Architecture, University of Virginia.
1957	Moved to Sarasota. Employed by Victor Lundy, Architect.
1958	Employed by Ralph and William Zimmerman, Architects, Sarasota.
1959	Returned to University of Virginia. Received Bachelor of Architecture degree, 1959.
1960	Received architectural registration in Florida.
1960–1961	Employed by Ralph and William Zimmerman, Sarasota.
1961	Established personal architecture practice, Sarasota.
1966	Plymouth Harbor, St. Armands Key, Sarasota (with Louis Schneider).
1969	Sandy Cove, Siesta Key, Sarasota (with James Holliday and James Durden).
1976–1981	Branch Office in Charlottesville, Virginia.
1983	McGuffey Hill Condominiums, Charlottesville, Virginia (with Carl Landow).
1984	United States Garage/Office renovation, Sarasota.
1986–1990	Ventana, residence for Anne and Frank Folsom Smith, Sarasota.
1991	AIA Florida/Caribbean Region *Test of Time* Award for Plymouth Harbor, St. Armands Key.
1961– present	Private practice, Sarasota.

Ralph Spencer Twitchell

1890   Born July 27, Mansfield, Ohio. Parents Alfred and Ellia C.

        (Downs) Twitchell.

1903   Enrolled in Rollins School (later College), Winter Park, Flor-

        ida. Family alternated between Ohio and Florida. Diploma,

        1910.

1910   Attended McGill University, Montreal, in architecture.

1912   Entered Columbia University, New York, which taught the

        Beaux-Arts method.

1913   Returned to Winter Park, Florida, for health reasons.

1915   Resumed architectural studies at Columbia University.

1916   Summer internship with architectural firm of Chatton and

        Hammon, Cleveland, Ohio (required by Columbia Uni-

        versity).

1917   Enlisted in Aviation Section, U.S. Army.

1918   Deployed to France as aviator; volunteered as test pilot. A

        plane he was testing crashed at Issouden, France, July 13,

        1918. Hospitalized for many months after.

1919   Returned to Columbia University; Bachelor of Architecture

        degree, 1920, Master of Architecture, 1921.

1921   Married Lucienne Glorieux, Port Chester, New York.

1922–1923 Employed by Carrere & Hastings and Raymond Hood, New

        York.

1923–1925 Returned to France where his in-laws lived. Then toured It-

        aly, where he studied Moorish and Spanish architecture.

1925	Summoned to Sarasota by Dwight James Baum, Architect, New York, to manage Baum's Florida office. Responsible for final construction of John and Mabel Ringling's mansion, Ca'd'Zan, Sarasota, 1925–1926.
1925	Registered in New York State.
1926	Left Baum's office. Depression comes early to Florida.
1927–1935	Spent summers in Salisbury and Lakeview, Connecticut. Completed neoclassical residential projects in New England, New York, and New Jersey. Wintered in Sarasota.
1936	Established his own architectural office in Sarasota. Formed Associated Builders, Inc., with Ed Root and nephews Larry and Jack Twitchell to provide design and construction services for clients.
1936–1937	Kantor residence, Siesta Key, Sarasota.
1937–1938	Showboat House, Lake Louise, Florida.
1938	Began experimenting with reinforced concrete decks and walls with John Lambie.
1938–1941	Influence of Frank Lloyd Wright from Florida Southern College, Lakeland, and Usonian residences became evident in Twitchell's work.
1940–1941	Lido Beach Casino completed, Siesta Key, Sarasota. Glorieux residence, Sarasota. Paul Rudolph employed for five months in Twitchell's office.
1941–1942	Twitchell residence, Big Pass, Siesta Key, Sarasota. Wheelan residence, Siesta Key.

1942–1945	Group Commander, Charleston Air Force Base, South Carolina, and Base Commander, Columbia Air Force Base, South Carolina.
1945	Returned to Sarasota. Big Pass architectural office designed and constructed.
1947	Paul Rudolph returned to office periodically while completing degree at Harvard.
1948	Twitchell-Rudolph associateship formed. Numerous residences were designed, of which Miller, Revere Quality House, and Healy ("Cocoon") guest house are best known of this period. The firm attained international recognition.
1949	Twitchell-Rudolph full partnership established.
1951	Twitchell-Rudolph partnership dissolved in March. Both Twitchell and Rudolph form their own Sarasota offices.
1953	Partnership with Jack West (dissolved 1954). Knott residence, Yankeetown, Florida.
1959–1965	Partnership with son Tolyn Twitchell. Twitchell residence. Circus residence, Siesta Key.
1969	Married Paula Bane after death of second wife, Roberta Finney Twitchell.
1978	Died January 30, Sarasota.

Tolyn Twitchell

1928	Born October 2, New York. Parents Ralph and Lucienne Twitchell.
1944–1947	Attended Hotchkiss School, Lakeville, Connecticut.
1948–1950	He and his brother Terry built Lucienne Nielsen's (formerly Twitchell) residence, Chilmark, Massachusetts.
1947–1953	Enrolled at Massachusetts Institute of Technology. Received Bachelor of Architecture degree.
1953–1956	Pilot, U.S. Air Force.
1956–1965	Partnership with Ralph Twitchell, Architect.
1956	Sylva Twitchell Hutchinson residence, Casey Key.
1957	Carlisle residence, Siesta Key.
1965	Received architectural registration in Florida.
1965– present	Tolyn Twitchell, Architect.

Jack West

1922	Born Galesburg, Illinois. Parents Harry Winfield and Mrytle Regina West.
1940	Enrolled at the University of Illinois in the engineering program.
1941	Volunteered for V12 Navy program. Graduated with B.S. in mechanical engineering, January 1944.
1944–1946	Attended naval officers' training school in New York. Duty with Navy in Pacific.
1946	Married Joyce Saville.
1946–1949	Entered Yale University School of Architecture. Received Bachelor of Architecture degree, 1949.
1949–1950	Employed with Twitchell and Rudolph, Sarasota.
1950	Received architectural registration in Florida.
1951	Private practice in Sarasota.
1951–1952	Employed by Pierra and Luckman, Los Angeles.
1952	Established office in Sarasota.
1953	Employed by Ralph Twitchell. Twitchell and West partnership formed a month later.
1953	Knott residence 2, Yankeetown, Florida.
1954	Tyler residence, Yankeetown, Florida. Twitchell and West partnership dissolved.
1954	Reestablished own office in Sarasota.
1956	West and Waters, Architects, partnership formed.
1958	Englewood Elementary School addition, Sarasota. Fruitville Elementary School addition, Sarasota. (Joint ventures with Bolton McBryde.)

1960   West and Waters partnership dissolved. J. West, Archi-

tect, AIA, and Associates formed.

1960   Tuttle Elementary School, Sarasota.

1964   Courtyard House for Arvida Corporation, Bird Key, Sara-

sota. Homes for Better Living Award.

1965   Sarasota City Hall.

1965   Sellew and West Associated Architects formed to do U.S.

Department of Housing and Urban Development work.

1966–   West and Conyers/Architects and Engineers partnership.

present

NOTES

 INTRODUCTION

1. William Rupp, interviewed by John Howey, 1993.

2. See "Residence in Sarasota," in *L'Architecture d'Aujourd'hui* 28 (February 1950), 98–99; the entire issue, "Walter Gropius et son école," was arranged by Rudolph, who also wrote the preface, p. 6. Also: "Maisons au bord de l'eau: habitation à Siesta Key, Californie [sic]," *L'Architecture d'Aujourd'hui* 49 (October 1953), 64–67; "House in Florida," *Architectural Review* 105 (June 1949), 287–290; Henry-Russell Hitchcock and Arthur Drexler, eds., *Built in USA: Post-War Architecture* (New York: Museum of Modern Art, 1952), 110–113; and "The Maturing Modern," *Time* 68 (July 2, 1956), 51, 56. A complete bibliography on Rudolph, including his work with Twitchell, is in Charles R. Smith, *Paul Rudolph and Louis Kahn: A Bibliography* (Metuchen, N.J.: Scarcrow Press, 1987).

3. Esther McCoy, *Modern California Houses: Case Study Houses 1945–1962* (New York: Reinhold, 1962), 9; see also "The Editor [John Entenza]", "Announcement: The Case Study Program," *Arts & Architecture* 62 (January 1945), 39: "That building, . . . is likely to begin again where it left off," and "the most important step in avoiding retrogression into the old, is a willingness to understand and to accept contemporary ideas."

4. Paul Rudolph, "Regionalism in Architecture," *Perspecta* 4 (1957), 12–19.

5. Paul Rudolph, interviewed by Michael McDonough, April 5, 1986; cited in McDonough, "The Beach House in Paul Rudolph's early Work," Master of Architectural History thesis, University of Virginia, 1986, p. 15.

6. "Bright New Arrival," *Time* 75 (February 1, 1960), 60.

7. Wolf von Eckardt, ed., *Mid-Century Architecture in America: Honor Awards of the American Institute of Architects, 1949–1961* (Baltimore: Johns Hopkins University Press, 1961), 198; "First Design Award, House, Siesta Key, Florida, Paul Rudolph, Architect," *Progressive Architecture* 65 (January 1955), 65–67.

8. To date no adequate study has appeared; selective sources include: "The Builder's House, 1949," *Architectural Forum* 90 (April 1949), 81–148; and "Best Houses under $15,000," *Life* 31 (September 10, 1951), 123–127.

9. Ned Eichler, *The Merchant Builders* (Cambridge: MIT Press, 1982), 86.

10. Roger Montgomery, "Mass-Producing Bay Area Architecture," in Sally Woodbridge, ed., *Bay Area Houses* (Laxton, Utah: Peregrine Smith, 1988), Ch. 5; and Susan Hall Harrison, "Post World War II Tract Houses: The Subdivision Developments of Joseph L. Eichler 1949–1956," Master of Architectural History thesis, University of Virginia, 1980.

11. Among many, see Tom Wolfe, *From Bauhaus to Our House* (New York: Farrar, Straus, Giroux, 1981); Peter Blake, *Form Follows Fiasco: Why Modern Architecture Hasn't Worked* (Boston: Atlantic/Little, Brown, 1977); Klaus Herdeg, *The Decorated Diagram: Harvard Architecture and the Failure of the Bauhaus Legacy* (Cambridge: MIT Press, 1983).

12. "Corbu Builds a Church," *Architectural Forum* 103 (September 1955), 120–128; and John Ely Burchard, "A Pilgrimage: Ronchamp, Raincy, Vézelay," *Architectural Record* 123 (March 1988), 171–178.

13. Paul Rudolph, "The Changing Philosophy of Architecture," *Architectural Forum* 101 (July 1954), 120–121; also in *AIA Journal* 22 (August 1954), 65–70. This was a paper Rudolph delivered at the AIA's annual convention in 1954.

CHAPTER ONE: **PHILOSOPHIES AND RESULTS**

1. Paul Rudolph, interviews by author, 1992–1994.

2. Ibid.

3. Ibid.

4. The Cocoon House appeared in *Kokusai Kentiku, L'Architecture d'aujourd'hui,* and the London *Architectural Review,* to name several international magazines.

5. Seventy-five people in the arts were known to be living on Siesta Key in 1950, according to Sarasota Department of Historical Resources records.

6. Periodically, design conferences have been held in Sarasota regarding this movement or to form the basis for other discussions on design. The most recent conference was held 15–17 July 1994.

CHAPTER TWO: **EARLY SARASOTA**

1. The mansion was named after Major Robert Gamble, a West Point graduate, whose Virginia family sent him to Florida to establish the sugar plantation.

2. Grismer, *The Story of Sarasota,* 105–109.

3. Ibid., 155–159, and Sarasota Department of Historical Resources records.

4. Hatton, *Tropical Splendor,* 49–56.

5. Weeks, *Ringling,* 116–126.

6. Paula Twitchell, interviews by author, 1992–1994.

7. Weeks, *Ringling,* 208–212.

8. Grismer, *The Story of Sarasota,* 243.

9. Paula Twitchell, interviews by author, 1992–1994.

10. Jack Twitchell, interviews by author, 1992–1994.

11. Phil Hammill, interview by author, 1993.

12. Phil Hammill, Chris Risher, and Paul Rudolph had all separately visited the Rosen-baum Residence by 1940.

CHAPTER THREE: **THE AWAKENING: 1941–1946**

1. Phil Hammill, interview by author, 1993.

2. Paul Rudolph, interviews by author, 1992–1994.

3. Ibid.

4. Paula Twitchell, interviews by author, 1992–1994.

5. Blake, *No Place Like Utopia,* pp. 38–39, 261–265.

6. Letter given to the author by Lu Andrews during a 1993 interview.

7. Paul Rudolph, interviews by author, 1992–1994.

CHAPTER FOUR: **THE BEGINNING: 1946–1948**

1. Paula Twitchell, interviews by author, 1992–1994.

2. Sylva Twitchell Hutchinson, interview by author, 1993.

3. Paul Rudolph, interviews by author, 1992–1994.

4. Ibid. The Denman house was destroyed to make way for a high-rise condominium.

5. Phil Hammill, interview by author, 1993.

6. Sylva Twitchell Hutchinson, interview by author, 1993.

7. Jack and Tolyn Twitchell, separate interviews by author, 1993 and 1994.

8. Paul Rudolph, interviews by author, 1992–1994.

CHAPTER FIVE: **RECOGNITION: 1948–1950**

1. Jack West, interview by author, 1994; the original $14,000 Revere house budget doubled to $28,000 when the house was built.

2. Tolyn Twitchell, interviews by author, 1994; Ralph Twitchell divorced his first wife, Lucienne, and married Roberta Healy Finney in 1950.

3. Gene Leedy, interviews by author, 1992–1994.

4. Ibid.

5. Ibid.

6. Mark Hampton, interviews by author, 1993–1994.

7. Sarasota Department of Historical Resources records.

8. Mark Hampton, interviews by author, 1993–1994.

CHAPTER SIX: **THE GATHERING: THE 1950S**

1. Both Jack West and Mark Hampton in Twitchell-Rudolph's office were likely involved in the detailing of the Leavengood residence.

2. The Sandering Beach Club was placed on the list of the National Register of Historic Places in 1994.

3. William Rupp, interview by author, 1993.

4. Written description by William Rupp given to author.

5. Design awards jury comments, *Progressive Architecture Magazine,* January 1955, 27–28.

6. Victor Lundy, interviews by author, 1993–1994.

7. Lundy won a Sarasota art competition with his painting of the Notre Dame cathedral, Paris. Syd Soloman and Carl Bickell were the jurors. This soon led to his Sarasota Chamber of Commerce building commision.

8. Victor Lundy, interviews by author, 1993–1994.

9. Bert Brosmith, interviews by author, 1993–1994.

10. Ibid.

CHAPTER SEVEN: **NEW DIRECTIONS AND DECLINE: THE 1960S**

1. Bert Brosmith, interviews by author, 1993–1994.

2. From author's 1993 tour of Sarasota schools.

3. Paul Rudolph, interviews by author, 1992–1994.

4. William Rupp, interview by author, 1993. Also see chapter 8, note 4.

5. Tim Seibert, interview by author, 1994.

6. Written description by Boyd Blackner given to author.

7. Boyd Blackner, interviews by author, 1994. Blackner moved from Sarasota in 1963 back to his home town of Salt Lake City, Utah, where he practices today. Besides Rudolph, he is the only other architect of the group to have won a National American Institute of Architects award for his work: the Kern's Building addition, 1978.

8. *Look Magazine,* May 1962, 17, 18, 66, 70–74.

9. Shirley Hiss, interview by author, 1993.

10. *Architectural Record,* May 1972, 37–38.

11. Paula Twitchell, interviews by author, 1992–1994.

12. Gene Leedy, interviews by author, 1992–1994.

13. Luce, speech reprinted in *Architectural Forum* 126, no. 5 (June 1967), 38–39. The speech was originally given by Henry Luce in May 1957 at the National American Institute of Architects convention in Atlanta, Georgia.

CHAPTER EIGHT: **BEYOND SARASOTA**

1. Kunstler, *The Geography of Nowhere,* 147–148.

2. Mildred Schmertz, interview by author, 1993.

3. Paul Rudolph, interview by author, 1992–1994.

4. William Rupp, interview by author, 1993. According to Rupp, this tower sketch was drawn by Rudolph in response to Rupp's query about what Rudolph thought a high-rise building should look like.

5. Victor Lundy has been with H.K.S., Inc. (formerly Harwood K. Smith, Inc.), Dallas, Texas, since 1984.

6. Peter Smithson, interviewed by author, 1993.

7. *Time,* January 11, 1993.

8. Ulrich Franzen, noted architect and Rudolph's fellow student at Harvard, observed: "He [Rudolph] started the first dialogue about architecture in the context of a city—this was a new approach to analyze problems of form and scale, space and function, as urban problems, rather than in the context of individual buildings."

9. Henry-Russell Hitchcock's description of Paul Rudolph in his review of Rudolph's premier exhibition of work in London.

BIBLIOGRAPHY

■ Arnade, Charles W. *The Architecture of Spanish St. Augustine*. Washington, D.C.: Academy of American Franciscan History, 1961.

Blake, Peter. *No Place Like Utopia: Modern Architecture and the Company We Kept*. New York: Alfred A. Knopf, 1993.

"Bold Structures Enclose Large Spaces at Low Cost." *Architectural Record* 138, no. 4 (October 1965), 177–188.

Bush, Donald J. *The Streamlined Decade*. New York: George Braziller, 1975.

Condit, Carl W. *The Chicago School of Architecture*. Chicago: University of Chicago Press, 1964.

Curl, Donald W. *Mizner's Florida: American Resort Architecture*. Cambridge, Mass.: MIT Press, 1984.

"Custom-House Winners." *House and Home* 15, no. 6 (June 1959), 113–129.

Federal Writers' Project of the Works Progress Administration for the State of Florida. *The WPA Guide to Florida: The Federal Writers' Project Guide to 1930s Florida*. Reprint, New York: Pantheon, 1984.

"Four Churches by Victor Lundy." *Architectural Record* 126, no. 6 (December 1959), 135–148.

Futagawa, Yukio, ed. *Paul Rudolph Architectural Drawings*. New York: Architectural Book Publishing Co., 1981.

Grismer, Karl H. *The Story of Sarasota: The History of the City and County*. Sarasota, Fla.: M. E. Russell, 1946.

Haas, Ronald W. *Classic Cracker*. Sarasota, Fla.: Pineapple Press, 1992.

Halberstam, David. *The Fifties*. New York: Villard Books, 1993.

Hatton, Hap. *Tropical Splendor: An Architectural History of Florida*. New York: Alfred A. Knopf, 1987.

Hiss, Philip. "What Ever Happened to Sarasota?" *Architectural Forum* 126, no. 5 (June 1967), 66–73.

Hitchcock, Henry-Russell, and Arthur Drexler, eds. *Built in USA: Post-War Architecture.* New York: Simon and Schuster, 1952.

Kunstler, James Howard. *The Geography of Nowhere: The Rise and Decline of America's Man-Made Landscape.* New York: Simon and Schuster, 1993.

LaHurd, Jeff. *Sarasota . . . A Sentimental Journey.* Sarasota, Fla.: Coastal Printing Inc., 1991.

Leung, Nora. *Experiencing Bond Centre.* Hong Kong: Studio Publications, 1990.

"The Lively Roofs of Victor Lundy." *Architectural Forum* 106, no. 6 (June 1957), 125–131.

Luce, Henry R. Speech (untitled). Reprinted in *Architectural Forum* 126, no. 5 (June 1967), 38–39.

Lundy, Victor. "Journey to the East." *Progressive Architecture* (December 1964), 134–145.

Lundy, Victor A. "A Place for Worship." *Architectural Record* 123, no. 7 (June 1958), 176–181.

Marquis, Alice Goldfarb. *Alfred H. Barr Jr.: Missionary of the Modern.* Chicago: Contemporary Books, 1989.

McCoy, Esther. Essay on John Entenza. In Barbara Goldstein, ed., *Arts and Architecture: The Entenza Years.* Cambridge, Mass.: MIT Press, 1990.

McQuade, Walter. "The School Board That Dared." *Architectural Forum* 110, no. 2 (February 1959), 79–87.

Norris, E. J. *Precast Concrete in Architecture.* New York: Whitney, 1978.

"Progress Report: The Work of Mark Hampton." *Progressive Architecture* 39, no. 6 (June 1958), 101.

"Resolutely Modernist." *Architectural Record* 177, no. 1 (January 1989), 74–85.

Rosenbaum, Alvin. *Usonia: Frank Lloyd Wright's Design for America.* Washington, D.C.: Preservation Press, 1993.

Rudolph, Paul. *Architecture and Urbanism,* no. 88 (July 1977).

Rudolph, Paul. *The Architecture of Paul Rudolph.* Introduction by Sibyl Moholy-Nagy. New York: Praeger, 1970.

Rudolph, Paul. *Paul Rudolph.* Introduction and notes by Rupert Spade. Photographs by Yukio Futagawa. New York: Simon and Schuster, 1971.

"The Sarasota School of Architecture." Convention issue. *Florida Architect* (September/October 1976).

"Sarasota's New Schools: A Feat of Economy and Imagination." *Architectural Record* 125, no. 2 (February 1959), 214–216.

Sergeant, John. *Frank Lloyd Wright's Usonian Houses: The Case for Organic Architecture.* New York: Whitney Library of Design, 1976.

Smith, Charles R. *Paul Rudolph and Louis Kahn: A Bibliography.* Metuchen, N.J.: Scarecrow Press, 1987.

Weeks, David. *Ringling: The Florida Years, 1911–1936.* Gainesville, Fla.: University of Florida Press, 1993.

West, Jack. *The Lives of an Architect.* Sarasota, Fla.: Faurve Publishing, 1988.

"Bold Structures Enclose Large Spaces at Low Cost." *Architectural Record* 138, no. 4 (October 1965), 177–188.

"Four Churches by Victor Lundy." *Architectural Record* (December 1959), 135–148.

House and Home 15, no. 6 (June 1959), 113–129.

Life (17 February 1941), 61–65.

Look 26, no. 2 (16 January 1962), 17–94.

"Progress Report: The Work of Mark Hampton." *Progressive Architecture* 39, no. 6 (June 1958), 101.

Progressive Architecture (January 1973), 89–91.

Progressive Architecture (January 1978).

Progressive Architecture (January 1988).

"Resolutely Modernist." *Architectural Record* 177, no. 1 (January 1989), 74–85.

"Sarasota's New Schools: A Feat of Economy and Imagination." *Architectural Record* 125, no. 2 (February 1959), 214–216.

"The Sarasota School of Architecture." Convention issue. *Florida Architect* (September/ October 1976).

"The Lively Roofs of Victor Lundy." *Architectural Forum* 106, no. 6 (June 1957), 125–131.

Time, 1993, pp.

ILLUSTRATION CREDITS

INDEX